RARE BIRDS

Rare Birds – #IFSHECANICAN
First publication 2015

Copyright © 2015 by Inspiring Rare Birds
Inspiring Rare Birds Pty Ltd
Level 2, 131 York Street, Sydney NSW 2000, Australia
www.inspiringrarebirds.com
Email: hello@inspiringrarebirds.com

Publisher – Jo-Ellen Burston
Lead writer and managing editor – Angela Gosnell
Executive creative director – Ivan Davies
Writer and editor – Dr Richard Seymour
Editor – Louisa McSpedden
Chief photographer – Jordan Kirk
Photographer's assistant – Eliza Ackland
Executive assistant – Megan Engard
Editorial assistant – Brodie Smith

Printed by immij, Australia.
Designed by evoagency.com.au
Thanks to Sydney Harbour Federation Trust.

Copyright to Inspiring Rare Birds Pty Ltd

ISBN 978-0-646-94648-1

A WORKBOOK TO INSPIRE YOU ON YOUR BUSINESS JOURNEY

RARE BIRDS

This Book belongs to....

Name

Address

Date

INTRODUCTION

This book documents the stories of a small group of amazing women entrepreneurs. No doubt you'll be amazed and inspired, as I am, by their journeys and insights. It's our second collection of extraordinary women. Our first, *Australia's 50 Influential Women Entrepreneurs*, brought together pioneers and influencers. I've called this second book *#IFSHECANICAN,* because I want it to be more than just a second collection of inspiring women – I hope it will also challenge and guide you on your own journey. These women are to be celebrated and cherished – they are role models and have much to share with us. They are my new friends and are courageous, vulnerable, abundance makers. They are Inspiring Rare Birds.

On reflection, much has changed from when I started my first business in 2006. Today, the possibilities for entrepreneurship are more obtainable than ever before. There have never been more resources, technology platforms or access to finance for entrepreneurs. Whether in Australia, Asia, North America or India, more women are starting more businesses, growing them more successfully, and creating more impact than ever before. But we know, if Australia is to flourish we must take more care to support and encourage entrepreneurs to start, establish, and build their businesses.

Someone I find enormously inspiring is the great American artist Twyla Tharp. She said, "In dreams, anything can be anything, and everybody can do. We can fly, we can turn upside down, we can transform into anything". Establish who you want to be before defining what you want to do or how you will go about doing it.

The stories here are about everyday young women, but these women have passion, and they are doing extraordinary things. Some are still finding their feet, others are trying to keep them despite rapid growth trajectories, and a few are observing their local and global impacts. The common theme in all of these stories is the real desire for a better world through social and economic impact, what I refer to as 'profitable smart heart'. The creativity, innovation and value creation we witness in Generation Y and Millennials will become the 'new' business models of the future. Let's learn from their problems as well as their solutions.

In this book we explore what they are overcoming and how they do it. We hear about their mentors, their funders, advisors and supporters. I also think it takes a tribe to raise an entrepreneur. Tribes such as Inspiring Rare Birds form because many women and men want to help nurture and

support women entrepreneurs, and because many women entrepreneurs seek assistance.

This is not about women before men or men versus women, it is absolutely about diversity and inclusion. I welcome with open arms all entrepreneurs, government agencies, academics, industry leaders and supporters to the table. We must move closer together and have the conversations that celebrate our strengths and differences. All Australians need to form relationships that span industries if we are to embrace global opportunities for entrepreneurship.

On a personal level, I've been incredibly honoured and privileged to meet the next generation of Inspiring Rare Birds and to be part of their current and future journeys. There are hundreds more stories we could have shared in this book that would be no more or less spectacular than the stories of these 27 entrepreneurs. Fortunately, we have an online community where we can share all of these remarkable journeys and, along with these stories, women can be supported by our mentoring program, deal room, education and resources. Essentially, these are the tools that inspire us to get started and support us to get the job done.

I return to my purpose and dream that one day, when you ask a boy or girl who they want to be when they grow up, you won't be surprised when they reply, "I want to build a business that will change the world" or "I want to be my own boss". And I hope my legacy, and the legacies of everyone within the Rare Birds community, will help nurture that response and will enable children to believe
#ifshecanican

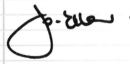

Jo Burston
Founder and CEO
Inspiring Rare Birds

www.inspiringrarebirds.com

7

CONTENTS

RARE
BIRDS

STEPH LORENZO

FOUNDER AND CEO OF PROJECT FUTURES

Project Futures has raised more than $3.2 million in the fight against human trafficking and slavery since Steph Lorenzo launched the not-for-profit in 2009. Her organisation runs the hugely successful annual Stella Fella Black Tie Ball in Sydney, but the 30-year-old says this isn't how she thought her life would turn out.

I was in Cambodia on a charity cycle challenge when I started reading Somaly Mam's autobiography *The Road of Lost Innocence*. She was exploited as a child – abused, raped, trafficked – yet she has been able to achieve great things in her life. It sparked something in me. In 2009, I organised a bike ride through Cambodia and 21 people joined me on it. We raised $80,000 for her cause.

In June that year I registered Project Futures as an organisation. Organising that bike ride wasn't super hard. I thought, 'surely I'm not the only one who wants to do fun events for a cause I was so passionate about?' and I wasn't. We held the bike ride year after year. We also had a party every year and then the parties grew.

The first two years we were solely focused on supporting Somaly's work in Cambodia and convinced her to come to Australia to share her story, and in 2010 she did. We organised a week-long itinerary of media events, two book signings, a university lecture, a corporate event and a young professional party. It was hard work, we were all volunteers running this week-long campaign and I even had to take an unpaid week off my real job, but it was pretty incredible. We got a taste of what it would be like getting corporate sponsors on board. I really loved showcasing the story of someone who inspired me. On a larger level, I also wanted to inspire people around me. It just sort of took off from there.

This path chose me

I don't think I ever thought to myself, 'I want to be an entrepreneur'. I thought I wanted to climb the corporate ranks and become the CEO of an advertising agency by the time I was 30 years old.

Now, not a day goes by when I don't think about Project Futures – even if it's on a weekend or at 12 o'clock at night. In my previous jobs I came in at 9am and went home at 5pm. I 'switched on' and 'switched off', whereas you can't switch off when you've got your own thing going on and you want it to be a success. You have to be careful not to burn out though. I want to maintain my energy levels, but I also want to maintain momentum.

Project Futures has been around for six years. I've only worked in the organisation in a full-time paid capacity for the past two years and we're only starting to build up our team now. We have three full-time staff. Even though we have had six years under our belt, only the past two years have really been in startup mode, as before we were all volunteers.

Our mission from the beginning hasn't been just about raising funds, it has also been about raising awareness, generating interest in young professionals and other Australians for a cause that affects us all.

WE LIVE HERE...

We formed our board first

It's essential to have a board if you're starting a not-for-profit. At the beginning we had six people on ours, including an accountant, a lawyer, an investment banker and a marketing director. Good legal and accounting work comes at a cost, but we got people on our board who loved what we were about and wanted to contribute. My motto is, 'you don't ask, you don't get' and everyone on our board, apart from my friend Steve and I, were all parents' friends or my old boss – people we knew would add value, expertise and clout that we needed. That's how we got Project Futures off the ground.

Building relationships is key to getting people on side, but you have to be genuine and authentic about it. I shouted all sorts of people coffees and drank so much of it myself, so I could get advice, guidance and understand this world I was getting myself into. The conversations were not only insightful, but so interesting. As humans we never stop learning and I always maintain that attitude. It's never just about the charity, it's never one-sided. The best relationships you maintain are the ones where you can also help the other person in some way.

Not everyone I spoke to wanted to get involved. They would always support me, but I didn't make them feel guilty about saying 'no'. I felt like that approach was always best. It might have taken more time, but we built our brand on that premise, of charity being something people *wanted* to be a part of as opposed something they *needed* to be part of or felt *guilty* about being a part of. It's hard work and it doesn't happen overnight that's for sure.

We recently had a board review to bring in new board members and it was great timing because we needed people who could help us move forward. I don't think a board determines the success of your organisation, but they play a crucial role in helping you with corporate governance.

I really respect all my board members. They're crucial in helping us formulate our strategy. A lot of not-for-profit board members just want to put the title on their resume. While I understand that not-for-profit board members do this work in their spare time and they're volunteers, anyone who is considering being on a board has to realise that if they agree to do it, then they have to really commit to it, so the organisation can continue to grow and succeed.

We've created a great community of people

When we launched, we organised one or two events a year. We used our 'gift of the gab' to secure venues and asked friends of friends if their bands could play for free or if they would DJ for nothing, and we charged for party tickets at the door.

There was always a risk something would go wrong, but we were so determined. We had a great group of young advisors who were influencers in their own network, so we motivated them to take ownership of it, and then execute the idea.

Creating a great community of people is what has also made the Stella Fella campaign and the highly anticipated Black Tie Ball such a success. But every single event we have done – it doesn't matter if there's 20 people there or 750 people – they all have a great vibe about them. There's a great willingness and want to do something for others, but also to have fun in that process.

We have hundreds of volunteers and we thrive in raising funds and awareness about human trafficking, and services that are provided to people who are victims of that.

When I'm working with people, I don't like to have anything fester or bubble. I'm not a micromanager (well I try not to be). I trust the people who work with me, but I also want to maintain a certain standard. I believe in being open, honest, authentic and transparent in everything I do and I like to lead by example. I really think that's something that drives me. For example, I've always bought a ticket to our own events, I've fundraised on a personal level and I am a recurring donor to my charity and also two others. I think it says that I believe in the cause just as much as other people do.

Getting paid for what I do

I fought being a paid employee of Project Futures for a long time, because in my mind it was always my side gig and I also knew I would probably never earn as much money working in the not-for-profit world as I would using my degree in marketing and communications.

In the third year our board said they would back me if I wanted to take on a full-time role in the organisation. Up until then I had been working in a full-time job and running Project Futures in my spare time. They thought I was working way too many hours.

I finally agreed to three days a week and funnily enough I totally undersold myself and was getting paid more working two days a week in the for-profit world than working three days in the not-for-profit world (not to mention the countless late nights and weekends). I thought I would do it for a year and a half and see how it went. I loved it and guess what? Our organisation grew and revenue grew, which meant the money we could give to our service partners also grew.

After a year and a half of working three days a week, I created a three year strategy with the help of an amazing mentor and also proposed to grow the team. We couldn't do that off the smell of an oily rag. If you want to get the best people you have to pay well or at least be competitive and not fall on the idea of just 'getting people with a good heart' to be involved. While all of our staff have left well paying jobs in the for-profit world to get paid less, the value they get is much more. They have ownership of what they do, can work flexible hours and they're part of a fun, vibrant team working for a great cause.

Looking back, I probably should have bit the bullet and got a full-time role sooner. I feel we would probably be miles ahead of where we are now if that had happened, but I was so afraid of criticism. Many people think 'administration' is the demon line item in a budget, but how can you do well without great people? And why should the not-for-profit sector – which is trying to solve some of the world's biggest problems – be devoid of the kind of talent employers in the for-profit world would pay for? We still struggle with this, but I feel our results speak for themselves.

We've been through some tough times

I have this amazing mentor who was high up in the banking industry and has done so much for us in a voluntary capacity. She really helped me believe we could grow. She came in at the perfect time, when we were growing rapidly and our revenue was almost doubling every year. She really helped lay the foundations for that. She's was really strong in financial forecasting and she pushed me personally, and professionally.

We went through a pretty tough time during the last half of 2014. One of our beneficiary partners received a lot of negative media. A member of staff also resigned due to personal reasons. It was our busiest time and I remember calling my mentor and saying I was going to quit.

She sat me down and went through the issues. I was so nervous that I wasn't going to deliver on the numbers, the budgets and the events, and all of those sort of things that we were trying to organise. I felt like we were going to let our beneficiaries down. But she said, 'don't let one small thing ripple into a bigger thing. Don't let it break the past five or six years of everything that you've done. You've still got your supporters; you've still got stuff happening; you've still got a lot of people who care about you'.

Sometimes you need that sense knocked into you. It's okay to have a bit of a shit time in business or charity, or whatever you're doing, and it's not a failure, it's just a learning curve.

We've raised millions of dollars so far

In the past financial year we raised just on $1,016,000. Our goal was a million, so we were really happy. We have raised over $3.2 million in the past six years. We support the Salvation Army Safe House for Trafficked Women, and Child Wise's National Child Abuse Helpline. In Cambodia, AFESIP Cambodia has a safe house run by Somaly Mam and we recently took on a new beneficiary, the Cambodian Children's Trust.

Now we're in the process of working out our new three to five year strategy. We see ourselves potentially working more closely with our beneficiary partners, going national and trying to create more engaged groups within different states. We've already branched out to Melbourne and the ACT.

We're also looking at going into some social enterprise ventures to allow some revenue streams to remain sustainable, so we don't have to rely on just donor and individual funding. We're focusing on new ways to remain sustainable and ahead of the game, and we're thinking about who we can partner and collaborate with. If we're going to stay current, fresh and new we need to seek out interesting innovative opportunities. I find it quite exciting, but it's going to be interesting getting that across to our board, which includes some extremely risk averse individuals, but that's all part of the journey I would say!

Big business wants to be aligned with us now

I've noticed that there's a growing focus on the person who is driving the cause. Corporates want the CEO or the person in charge, but then they ask, 'what are your overheads and what's your salary?' and they want it to be at a certain level, but they're sort of propping you up as this inspiring young female leader.

So I feel there's a real disconnect. It's frustrating, because it has been ingrained in us for so long that charities have to run off the smell of an oily rag to be successful. People don't realise that charities need longevity and consistency as much as businesses do. If corporates really want to authentically engage with us it has to be long-term, sustainable and driven by relationships. Companies would never chop and change their lawyers or accountants. They would never want their staff to chop and change, so why is it that companies constantly say, 'every six months we choose these new charities to support'? I know there are reasons for it, but they can never really fully engage with that charity and see great work achieved over a long period of time and that's a shame.

We're so lucky

I'm so lucky to live in Australia and when I think of people in my network, I think they're lucky too. We need to stop thinking about ourselves and start thinking about people who really need a hand. We need to work to support them or help them in some way, so they can feel as lucky as we do. That's why I'm pouring my life into Project Futures. I'd like to be remembered as someone who cared about people; cared about the world.

I do think about the kind of person I want to be remembered as. What kind of legacy do I want to leave behind? I'd love for people to remember me as a kind-hearted person, who wants to give back to communities that are vulnerable. I'd love to inspire other people, like my friends and the people around me to do the same, but not in guilt-trip kind of a way – more in an inspiring and positive way.

Steph's tips for nailing it

• **Board members play a significant role in your organisation, because you report to them. You have to be confident they'll make the right decisions and have the best interests of the organisation at heart. Try to drive the agenda in meetings, but be flexible. Don't get caught up in political red tape like so many other charities do.**

• **The not-for-profit world is so saturated. You have to look at where your point of difference is and look at the market. Do something that's different and disruptive. If you don't, then work with an entrepreneur or a charity that does. And if you do have something that's really different then go for it. Get the best people to support you and use your resources and networks wisely. People underestimate how hard it is and how long it takes.**

For example, in 2015, our Stella Fella Ball, sold out in a month! That's 750 people and we also had people on waiting lists. It has taken five years to achieve that kind of success. There has to be that authenticity behind everything you do and you have to work hard at it every single day. I don't want to scare people away from doing it, but that's the truth.

Steph's vision and competence

Project Futures has purpose. As Steph says: having an altruistic purpose can be a double-sided sword. Some people generously gift their support to such an organisation (for example, the board and supporters who volunteer their time and expertise). However, others seek to engage with such organisations through an exchange transaction (for example, corporates choosing where donated money is used or communicated).

To scale, Project Futures will need to understand the implications of these sometimes conflicting (sometimes complementary) gifts and exchanges. This understanding will directly impact the vision and competence of the organisation, which will in turn inform Project Futures' strategy. It will also impact the way the organisation engages with stakeholders, such as corporates.

I'D LIKE TO BE REMEMBERED AS SOMEONE WHO WAS ALWAYS THERE TO HELP PEOPLE.

What can I learn from Steph Lorenzo?

ROSIE O'HALLORAN

FOUNDER AND CEO FOUNDATIONS.(AU) AND THE INSTITUTE FOR GLOBAL WOMEN LEADERS AND CREATOR OF THE HEARTWORKS PROGRAM

Photographer: Damian Bennett

When Rosie O'Halloran went to Uganda and was confronted with children living on the street, she knew that she had to do something to help. At that point her not-for-profit organisation, foundations.(au), was born. Her driven nature and social consciousness has helped her become a social entrepreneur, also co-founding the Institute for Global Women Leaders and developing heartworks, a program to support young women in their personal development.

In late 2008 I was watching television one night when I saw a landscape of green hills flash across the screen. I had this urge to go to that place, so I rang the ABC to find out where it was located. Turns out those hills were in Uganda, so I bought a plane ticket and headed straight there. When I first arrived in Uganda I had a deep sense that my feet knew where they were walking that whole trip. It just felt like home. I came back to Australia feeling like I needed to do something more to support the people I had met there.

I set up the non-profit foundations.(au) in Australia, so I had a structure behind me for when I returned to Uganda. I went back and did research with a friend, surveying families in the community to get a better understanding of how we might be able to assist. We came across a group of kids who didn't have any immediate family taking care of them and some of them were living on the street. They inspired me to open an orphanage at the end of January, 2010.

I have learnt so much about myself and the world since then. In 2014, I co-founded the Institute for Global Women Leaders and have started working on a new program for teenage girls. Though the projects I have worked on are all so different, each experience has taught me something new and helped me build my skill-set to be able to help others.

I want to empower women to know their full potential

There were two reasons I started the Institute for Global Women Leaders. One was my own journey as a young woman running a non-profit. I found it really challenging to be part of the social entrepreneur space. I sought out a lot of support by enrolling in different programs or seeking mentors, but I couldn't always find what I was looking for. I connected with other women doing similar work and they were saying similar things. There was a need for an organisation to exist that could specifically support young women social entrepreneurs.

The other reason sprang from an experience in Uganda. The first child that we supported to go to school was a girl called Abbias. When we met Abbias she'd finished primary school, but she wasn't able to start high school because her parents couldn't afford it. We were supporting her to go to high school, and about halfway through she became sick.

We took her to the doctors and thought that she would be okay. The local doctors weren't able to help her so we suggested sending her to the capital city to see a specialist. We fundraised and were able to send her and her mum up to the capital city, Kampala.

When they were at the hospital the doctor did a couple of initial tests on her, and then basically said, 'You're just a girl from a village and you don't matter'. He sent her home and six weeks later she died.

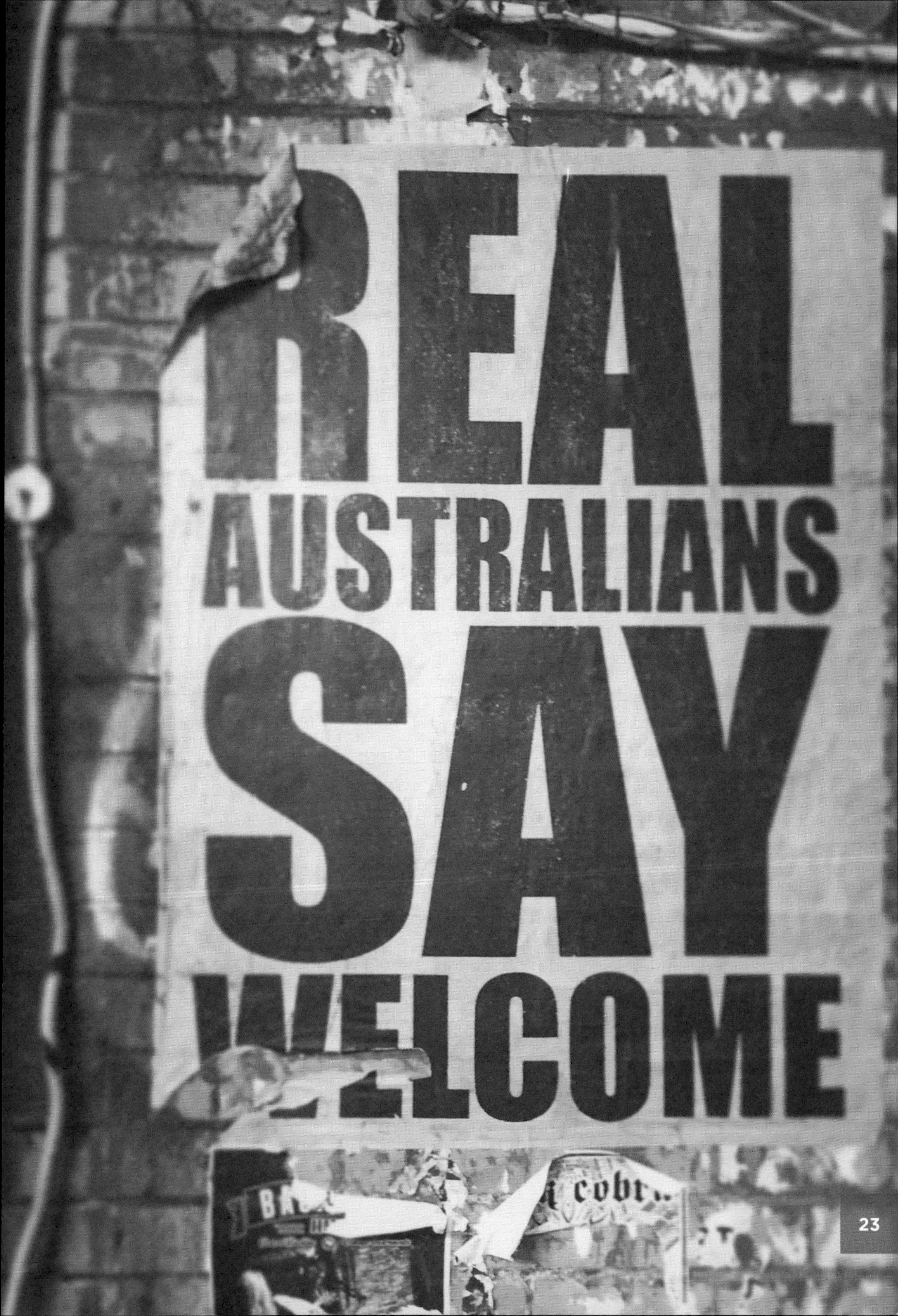
REAL
AUSTRALIANS
SAY
WELCOME

I was really confronted by that experience and I couldn't believe someone could tell a girl she didn't matter. Losing my friend Abbias inspires my desire for young women to know they have worth in this world. The Institute for Global Women Leaders aims to help encourage and empower young women to be strong and fearless in the face of adversity across the world.

I didn't have a consistent income for five years

For the first five years I didn't have a consistent income. I just did odd jobs. I put everything into foundations.(au), but if I could go back and change things I would have done things differently. That's partly because at times I was really struggling financially – thankfully I always had a safety net in my family. The bigger reason was a surprise to me: I internalised a lack of income as a lack of self-worth.

A huge challenge of running a non-profit is just making sure you've got enough money coming in. Traditionally, not-for-profits rely on the generosity of others. That's not a consistent funding source. At times in Uganda I had to make decisions despite not always being certain of what our budget would be. When I started my new business I got involved with a financial services firm dedicated to entrepreneurs. They structured my new business so I was finally earning an income and when that happened I burst into tears. That change has had a huge impact on my sense of self worth.

The process of running a non-profit has made me question so many things about charities and the way that we do non-profit type activities in Australia. I would like to see non-profits that work in a similar space coming together to share resources and create a bigger impact. My current work is moving into the social entrepreneurial space.

Transitioning away from foundations.(au) was emotional

I never envisaged the foundations.(au) orphanage to be a permanent solution for the children. While the home has provided a safe and loving place for the children to grow, we have worked hard to build the capacity of the community so that one day they could be the ones providing these children with a safe and loving home. I am currently in the process of transitioning the children into local care arrangements and I'm focused on finding more community based, permanent solutions for each of them.

Fundamentally, we're still providing finances for these children to go to school, but the organisation is working much more on a local level, with the children's caregivers making the day-to-day decisions. This transition has been emotional for me. I have been heavily invested in the organisation and feel deeply connected to these kids so it has been a difficult process to go through personally.

Now I am focusing on a new project – a concept I developed in 2014, called heartworks. It is a personal discovery program to assist young women in the transition from being an adolescent to a young adult. This concept won me the InStyle and Audi Style Scholarship, which allowed me to further develop the program. Melbourne Girls Grammar School in Victoria bought a school version of the program for their Year 11 students, which was a huge milestone. I am developing the program as an e-course and working on a retreat in Bali that will explore the same program principles.

Self-belief is a constant battle

Throughout this journey I have battled with a lack of self-belief and faced many fears. I've built internal strength and resilience as a result of the hurdles I have overcome. It's a continual process of learning and growth. Often I have felt like I don't have the formal qualifications to do what I do, but now I am at a stage where I feel like my experiences are my credibility.

Each day I work on my self-belief and at times push myself to keep on going. I'm driven by courage, freedom and integrity. They're my three core values. My business mantra is, 'your life is a work of heart'. I put my heart and soul into everything I do.

My personal purpose is about loving. It's about really knowing what that is and having that experience in life. 'To know love, to be love and to share love' is my personal mantra. That language is sometimes challenging to bring out in a corporate or business space – I'm still trying to figure out how to do that.

I'm driven to make the world a better place. Once we move into that space of personal transformation within ourselves the ripple effect can lead to really deep social change. I have been able to actively make a difference in the lives of others, whether it is the children in Uganda or other women social entrepreneurs. Giving back is so important, but you have to be resilient as an entrepreneur in order to be successful. I'm committed to my own growth and learning, and then facilitating and assisting others.

Getting support is so important

I do a lot of personal learning. When I first started foundations.(au) I had basic knowledge of things like financial literacy and pitching for funding so I have taught myself a lot, but I've also been part of entrepreneurial groups and that has helped.

I was selected to participate in a program called Young Social Pioneers, which is run by the Foundation for Young Australians. It's a 12-month leadership development program for young people running social purpose organisations. Being part of a group of like-minded people experiencing the same problems and challenges as me was really valuable. It gave me confidence and fostered a community.

I have learned a lot from my mentors, one of whom connected with me because she had seen what I was creating and wanted to be part of bringing it to life. She has been instrumental in her strategic advice and has assisted with my growth by introducing me to other key people.

I'm a bit of a dreamer, though I'm getting better at being more pragmatic: because I'm learning I have to be. I do have a very idealistic view of the world; there's a big part of me that wholeheartedly believes that world peace is possible. I just make sure that I've got people around me who can support me and help me to look at things from different perspectives.

Rosie's tips

Trust in yourself, in the process, and in the bigger picture. Learn who you are – what drives you, what inspires you, what challenges you. Stay true to what's true for you. Know it's okay to say 'no'. It's okay to disagree. It's okay to change your mind. Be patient with yourself and with others. Whatever it is you do, do it with joy. Spend time reflecting, dreaming, meditating, then go out there and make it happen. The planet needs what you've got so step up, show up and shine. Find your tribe. Give thanks. And bring the love. It's all going to be okay.

Rosie's vision and competence

Rosie highlights the core challenge facing most organisations – meshing an enterprise's resources and capabilities (or competencies) with its vision (also referred to as its mission or purpose). This challenge can be considered more personally, the entrepreneur can address the questions, 'what can I do?' and 'who can I become?'

We know that some entrepreneurs prioritise the vision, spending a lot of effort in its articulation and documentation (often also adding related statements of mission, values and purpose).

Other entrepreneurs seem to prioritise the consideration of resources and capabilities (addressing questions such as, 'what can I start with now?' or 'what will ensure I can make do with what I have?'). It may well be better to do away with these prioritisations – try to answer these questions of 'doing' and 'becoming' concurrently, as they are in many respects inseparable. Rosie's later ventures seems to acknowledge and advise this.

I'VE BUILT INTERNAL STRENGTH
AND RESILIENCE AS A
RESULT OF THE HURDLES
I HAVE OVERCOME.

IT'S A CONTINUAL PROCESS
OF LEARNING AND GROWTH.

What are my thoughts on this?

9

GEN GEORGE

FOUNDER AND MANAGING DIRECTOR OF ONESHIFT

OneShift is an online talent marketplace that connects local candidates with local businesses. Its founder Gen George raised $5 million dollars a few months after launching and believes its four values are what keeps everyone inside OneShift firmly focused on achieving their vision.

The idea for OneShift came from a problem I had, trying to find work that suited my schedule. A lot of my friends were also having the same issue. I tried to help them and then it grew into thinking about how I could get more people into work and change the way candidates choose to work.

The first year of the business was self-funded between my partner in crime (my father Phil George) and myself. We launched on 13 June, 2012, and our first customer was a hotel in Woollahra. I was working at a property company as a team assistant and every night after work and at the weekend I would hit the main shopping streets or universities with an iPad, convincing students, business owners and managers to sign up.

We made it work with smoke and mirrors

My first blog claimed to be a site that had a matching algorithm that 'magically' matched people instantly with jobs but, in fact, it was me staying up all hours manually connecting bartenders to bar jobs. The idea was for people to find one-off shifts, but I technically didn't know how to build that functionality, so I used what I had to make it work and created a blog called Sneaky Shifts. I started posting as many shifts as businesses would allow. I did this by calling the businesses or turning up on the weekend and saying, 'just give me the job, then you can join our marketplace'.

I got candidates to sign up by hitting the Sydney universities with posters and social media. Every night after work, I used to print posters and cover the universities from end to end using duck tape. Yes, it was pretty unprofessional.

When we first started, the idea was for you to be able to do one-off shifts behind the bar on a Friday night, so you could go out on Saturday night. Now, we've really adapted it to focus on data and behavioural analytics from our users, such as what skill sets users have; the live data of supply and demand in any one postcode; what jobs they are looking for, and how they react when looking at roles. One of the challenges is trying to keep up with what people are actually using the marketplace for and adapting the concept, brand and model to suit that.

In the first week of December, 2012, OneShift had a full page-article in a leading financial newspaper and a two-minute segment on a TV current affairs show. Within days we were approached by Programmed Integrated Workforce (ASX: PRG) to invest in the company. We raised $5 million for 27.5 per cent of the business, valuing us at around $20 million when we were about a year old. They've been our only investors, so it's us and them.

Then, in 2013, we finally built a payment gateway and could start playing with the business model. With a big grin on my face, I called the hotel's manager: 'Guys, you're going to have to start paying for this now'. And, of course, the system had a bug and it wasn't the smoothest of sales calls, but we got there in the end.

The first OneShifters

The first person we hired was a backpacker called Jade, who we found through OneShift. We grew the business organically. The whole process was really about filling up my day as much as possible, then handing over my whole day's work to someone, so I could keep looking for growth opportunities. Because we've grown like that I don't have to be involved in every single thing that's going on.

We also had the benefit of having a chief financial officer involved in the business really early on. Their skill set has been critical to the success of the company, as it has provided mentorship and education about this aspect of business.

There are about 50 of us in OneShift now. It's continually changing and evolving, and every day is different. Our vision is to change the way people choose to work. Whether it is one hour a week or 100, we want to give people choice in their lifestyle. Today that means for us to provide a platform or community where people can plug and play skill sets, work and experiences to suit what they need at that time. For example, this could mean booking a flight through us, getting short term accommodation in New York, working three weeks at a job and then doing an online graphic design course to pick up extra work to pay for that next flight to London.

It's quite a big vision, however, one of our values is test, fail, learn. This means we are constantly testing different options and if we fail we learn from this, and then adapt the business and the vision. It is important to remain agile because, let's be serious, no one really knows the right answer.

We are always looking for better ways to scale the business more effectively and faster. We are not necessarily looking for money though. It's about what investors can bring to the table that can grow this business 100 times quicker. Even if investors wanted to give us $100 million, it would still be about them being able to guarantee traction, because at the end of the day there's no guarantee with cash.

Our audience is quite broad. We have people aged from 16 to 86. Our eldest user is 86 (going on 46, according to her profile), who pulls shifts at a retirement home, has a Certificate III and IV in Aged Care, and hangs out with the business's 'clients'. We want to create a place where introductions happen for work that would never have happened before. For example, we have a policeman who is saving up to pay for his fiancé's dream wedding. Cool stories like that enable people to do things they couldn't have done before we launched.

We have team meetings and we set goals

We have a once a week CORE team kick-off with managers of each team. This session is about clear visibility around what each team is focusing on for that week and clear task-driven KPIs. We manage this through Trello, so we are all across items as they progress, so we can remain agile across the whole team.

We also have an end of month company meeting, where it's really about getting that bigger picture and looking at what each department achieved in the past 30 days, and what KPIs we have for the next 30 days or the next quarter. We also see if there were any stuff-ups and have a good giggle at those, so we all learn from it. The purpose of all this is transparency throughout the whole business. If we have a whole team heading in the same direction, for the same purpose, then we have a better chance of getting there.

Our values are: 'no bullshit', 'make it happen', 'team or family first', and 'test, fail, learn'. We try to make sure everyone is enabled so they're in line with those. Our culture is flat structured. It doesn't matter if you're the receptionist or the chairman, you're going to affect the direction of the business. That's why we have so many whole team get togethers. I still have one-on-ones with the whole business once a quarter, as this means I can get direct and honest feedback from everyone's experience within the business. We've got to keep pushing and changing, and we can only do that from the top I guess.

Failure isn't necessarily a bad thing either. You stuff up, you learn, and you evolve. I'd never change anything that has happened along our journey, just because whatever we have been through – the good, the bad and the ugly – has made us who we are and what we are today.

Some HR managers tell me to bugger off

I'm used to being in situations where we've got to pitch the business to HR teams who get to say, 'yes' or 'no' if they want to use us, and they can be the most critical people.

I'm frank with them and say, 'this is what I'm trying to achieve. I want a relationship where we can give each other feedback about what works and what doesn't work. Start using it and tell me what you think. I've got thick skin – let's make this truly work for you'.

Ninety five per cent of the time they say, 'great, fantastic, love it, let's roll this out'. Other times we get feedback and the developers get involved, and they roll out the changes as quickly as possible. People love that we can turn to our developers and say, 'hey, no one likes the blue button, change it to green, quick'.

The scary thing about HR teams is they can change every six months. I've pitched to customers who have basically told me to bugger off and I'm like, 'okay, see you in six months when you're not here'. And unfortunately that's the way it is. In this business, there are early adopters and people who want to stick their heels in the ground, because they feel you are trying to replace them with a robot. And that's fine.

The most innovative companies and teams in the world are the ones that test constantly. I can come back and get buy-in from someone who wants to be an ambassador in six to 12 months' time, because it only works well if somebody is willing to put time into making the relationship work. As with anything.

Hiring is critical for business success

When I hire people cultural fit is more important to me than their skill sets or experience. For any newcomer to the business I make sure I interview them and get an understanding of who they are and what they are about. I think if your values are in line with your work ethic and your morals, and all those sorts of things, it all just falls into place, whether those skill sets are there or not. If they've got the right attitude they'll figure out how to make it work.

I meet people sometimes, who I think could be OneShifters and I'll say, 'come on in, we'll figure out a job'. We've done that a couple of times and it has worked out really well. Hiring is critical to the team and the business's success, because it doesn't matter how good your ideas are, it all comes down to the team driving it.

How we get the message out there

We have a communications manager in-house who produces a lot of content for LinkedIn, Twitter, our blog, and so on. We need to make sure we're relating to both sides of our audience and that includes a lot of different types of people who we need to be speaking to, and providing them with information they want and need. This is especially true when we work with journalists and are focused on getting the right stories out there in the media.

We also have a chief marketing officer, who is bringing his digital/stalking skills into the business. It's about continually up-skilling the organisation. As we develop and get a little more mature and know where we're heading, we're filling in gaps, so we can keep accelerating. Whether it's development, SEO, management, and so on – we just keep trying to improve.

It's about going back to those values of test, fail, learn, and asking ourselves, 'how can we do it better?' The biggest failure you can have as a business is to say, 'oh great, it's working', because that's short range vision. You need to go, 'how can we keep twisting, twisting, twisting, to get the most out of it?'

Collaborations are also one of the best ways for us to do quick tests and get maximum impact. Finding a business that specialises in what you want to try out, means you both get the benefit of scale and you are not deviating from your full focus being on your core product. Being extremely clear about expectations and what success looks like is, of course, really important. If it works then, 'great, let's get married, but let's dip our toes in the water first and get a feel for each other'.

The team's hard work and their ability to constantly challenge the status quo has got us to where we are. It hasn't taken one person, it has taken everyone in the room to get us to this point today. (Sneaky shout out to team OneShift!)

We've got an awesome referral system

We've got 175,000 likes on Facebook and we're on Twitter, and we get a lot of traction through LinkedIn. We've also got an awesome referral system from the sales team, so we get two or three referrals a week from any sort of business they're speaking to. One of our biggest focuses is making sure we have a small business mentality, but a big business reach. We have a one-on-one focus where you'll be called straight back – that sort of thing. It's important to get that feedback from people we talk to, so we can keep evolving.

When people say a business is an overnight success, they never mention the four or five years of slog and hard work behind it. The time you put into it is going to be evident in the output. Nobody has the right answers and nobody knows what the end looks like.

For us, it's about creating a platform where people can just 'plug and play' life, experiences, education and sort themselves out financially or support themselves financially while living life the way they want to. We really want to change the way people choose to work, which is pretty big 'blue sky' stuff.

I love doing this. It is work-life balance for me, because I'm doing something I'm passionate about. It's always changing and there are new challenges, new successes and complete and utter failures every day, which still continues to surprise me. I wouldn't be doing anything else.

Gen's advice for startups

• A lot of people don't realise that building a site doesn't mean people are going to use it, and getting funding doesn't mean you're successful. Actually trying to make that site work often comes down to doing things like physically sitting on the back end of the site until 3am matching people with the 'magic algorithm'. You're only as successful as the amount of physical work and time you put into it though. Blood, sweat and probably a glass of wine, then tears.

• A lot of startup entrepreneurs think funding answers everything. Getting funding is great, but the next thing is actually doing what you said you were going to do. Funding is just the beginning, because then you have to deliver and actually keep evolving.

Gen's vision and competence

Gen states the importance of a company's vision, and she recognises how a company's values and objectives relate to that statement. A vision typically states what a business does and what it could possibly be if it became the best version of itself. It should clarify, engender confidence, and inspire.

Although an organisation's vision and values fundamentally do not change, as Gen says, the objectives supporting that vision can shift, sometimes significantly. There are some questions that will help an entrepreneur understand whether a vision is appropriate: Firstly, does it utilise your competencies (your resources and capabilities)? That is, will it encourage you to do better at the things you already do well (if they are the right things to do)?

Secondly, does it look outside your business to external opportunities and the needs of customers, industry and the business's environment? That is, are you able to make a difference and have impact?

Thirdly, does your vision look towards what it is you really believe in? For example, is the vision yours, and is it a personal expression of your beliefs and dreams? Successful entrepreneurs believe in what they and their business stand for (rather than just what products it sells). They can use their vision to shape and articulate that passion, so their customers, employees, family and investors all see where the business is heading.

4

AIMEE MARKS

FOUNDER AND CEO OF TOM ORGANIC

Aimee Marks started a new conversation with women in Australia about one of the most intimate products they use: tampons. As CEO, founder and chief storyteller of TOM Organic, Aimee has not only created a range of certified organic sanitary products; she has created a lifestyle that encourages women to care about what they put in their bodies and, in turn, to look after the world.

TOM Organic is a values-based business that comes from such an authentic place. The idea came to me because I couldn't find organic female products anywhere. I wasn't able to source the product from a consumer perspective so I saw an opportunity and a need.

Our products create conversations

TOM Organic is a range of intimate products and that lends itself to intimate conversations. This covers everything from the most hilarious dinner party conversations and most intriguing phone calls and emails, to the conversations we have with the male buyers at supermarkets.

I feel that a lot of brands in our space take advantage of that intimacy and in some ways scare younger women and younger girls into feeling like a period is something that you need to plug up and ignore. Whereas for us, we really focus on talking about the lifestyle that sits around conscious buying choices in your life and one of those choices is TOM Organic.

If you're going to buy organic or natural cosmetics, food and produce then it's a normal thing to be thinking about the absorption of the chemicals that are in contact with the most intimate part of our bodies. It's a natural and normal conversation that we have that puts us on an intimate and trusting level with our community. To continue that level of trust we have had to work really hard at getting organic certifications and the right sort of distribution partners to practice what we preach.

Australian female consumers are some of the most savvy in the world and this is one of the hardest markets to be in and create success with products. Women also trust recommendations and look to influencers and friends for references. It's always been about creating a deep and one-to-one relationship with our consumers through word of mouth and having authentic conversations, not just about periods. We're factual about it, but we think that having an organic tampon and having a period is just all a part of life.

I feel we have a responsibility to have these conversations. We're not just talking about a product, we're talking about something that women use every single month, 12,000 to 15,000 times over their lifetime. The lifestyle we've created around the brand is something that women aspire to be a part of. The choices that every woman makes create an impact in their life and also in our world for future generations.

Everything about the business comes from my heart

There's such an incredible amount of hard work that goes into what I do. How can you deviate from what your heart says? It just doesn't work. As a business woman you've got to constantly evolve yourself, your business and your team. That comes from a place of being really honest and vulnerable with your own beliefs and values, which is something that is deeply ingrained in the heart of what we do. Values from home life do not need to be disjointed when you step foot into the office – it's all very much integrated. That set of values allows us to attract and keep good people, and continue to have honest, authentic conversations on a mass scale.

I started TOM Organic solo, but now we are a team of seven. We also work with a number of different outsourced companies. I have tried to keep the core values alive in the business with a lot of refinement around the types of people we bring in. They follow my lead and set a certain standard, level of energy and culture in the office, which has transpired across business decisions and strategy.

It has always been a dream of mine to create an effortlessly exciting workplace. This is tied to the product we are bringing to women and we all feel a responsibility to educate them about the choices that we once didn't know we had. It comes down to the core of our business: sourcing and providing women with the absolute purest female products that are on the shelves.

Every day is a challenge and an opportunity

In the early days it was an extremely small business. I was trying to grow it from my bedroom by selling to local businesses and pharmacies (with my Mum by my side supporting me unconditionally), and learning from my immediate local community of women what they wanted from TOM Organic. Together we grew the brand. It was two steps forward, one step back (and sometimes three). The products were stocked in 60 to 100 stores and I was working overtime on the side to keep the momentum going. I believe that if you have a backup 'plan B' you just don't make 'plan A' work, so I committed 110 per cent to making 'plan A' – TOM Organic – a feasible business. It was scary and I was vulnerable, but I had to take the risk. Every inch of me needed it to work. Failing wasn't an option.

At one point my bank account got down really low and times like that made me question everything. I asked myself, 'do I actually love what I'm doing? Is there really a need for this and is this really good for people?' What got me through is the knowledge that people really do need this. I really believed in what I was doing. It was an incredibly proud moment to finally get the product into the major supermarkets. It was really emotional, especially as these conversations were so deep and we needed it so badly.

While a lot of people think that getting stocked in a supermarket is like winning the lottery, for us the hard work started once we got on the shelves. It put us in a whole new stratosphere, with access to women in every inch of the country. We could really create that mass market brand in the health space that we dreamed of, but we also had a responsibility to really reach and talk to those women.

Capital investment helped us grow

I got to a point where I just knew that to scale and grow I needed capital. That was a big journey for me to go on, because I challenged myself to find impact money that also had non-financial value attached to it. I was pitching to lots of different venture capital groups, and angel investors, and talking to lots of mentors at the time. I realised when I met my business partners Small Giants, that it actually should feel like a really exciting step – not like you are losing part of your business, but growing as a whole together, because you're increasing the reach and impact.

The relationship instinctively felt right from the beginning. It even felt like family because we shared the same values ('Nobody ever achieved anything extraordinary on their own', is a quote I love). Tapping into and trusting your gut instinct is critical in business and I have a strong ethical compass. It's got to feel right every day since it's something you work so hard for. Once my partners came on board we were in a position where we were able to place our first order for Woolworths. It was a million dollar tampon order. How on earth could I have possibly done that on my own or with a partner who didn't quite have the values and heart?

Mentoring is so important

For me, mentoring works both ways – it's an opportunity for me to pass on what I have learnt and in return I always learn something new. The dream for me is to be able to short-cut some of the mistakes I've made, which in turn are part of some of the successes, with a view to helping fast track budding entrepreneurs. When I was starting the business one commitment I made was to make sure that I helped younger female entrepreneurs as well. The people who have mentored me have helped me get where I am, so I feel a responsibility to give back and mentor others. It's something I really enjoy doing.

When I was first starting the business my mentor was incredibly supportive. He was entrepreneurial and had the right mindset for someone who was challenging every possible status quo in business and products. Most importantly, he wasn't a 'yes' man. My Mum was also an incredible support and strength and so was my husband, who also runs his own company. Having a close family to back you is so important and I feel grateful for them, as it can be quite lonely starting a business.

When I got to a point where I was dealing with supermarkets, which was a whole new space, I was lucky to have the incredible support of fellow Australian-owned fast-moving consumer goods (FMCG) supermarket brands. Many are B Corporations and we work collectively to positively influence the business landscape in Australia for social and environmental good.

I've also been involved in business support networks, and without the guidance and support of my mentors I wouldn't be in the position I am today. Ultimately, they encourage me to listen to my instinct, while guiding me through their experiences and empowering me to understand that I know my business best, and should make decisions with that in mind.

I want to encourage people to pursue their dreams

Before I went on this journey I had just finished university and I was trying to get a job. I had the idea for TOM Organic and I really wanted to pursue it, but at the time it was a dream. I remember talking to my family friend, who must have seen something in the idea. I'd just come back from an interview with a global firm and had been sitting in a room with the most amazing view over the city. I remember the moment when I thought there was something else that I needed to be doing. That family friend ended up writing me a cheque for $10,000, which I used to design and create TOM Organic.

He said, 'I don't want to see this money again if it doesn't work out in 12 months, but if it does you can pay me back'. So I paid him back. Last year, I was involved in the Telstra Business Women's Award and I sat in the exact same room at the global firm and looked out at the same view. I felt a real responsibility to have the capacity to one day have those same conversations with young entrepreneurs who are at that intersection in their careers – those people who are wondering if they will be vulnerable and brave enough to pursue something they're passionate about. That's what that $10,000 investment meant to me.

Aimee's advice for entrepreneurs

Be selective about the kinds of people you want to work with every day. It's not just about the money, because you can go to a bank for that. It's about the people you want around your boardroom table; the people you want continually challenging you and the people you want to celebrate with. I am incredibly proud and grateful for everyone I work with at TOM Organic. They have had such a positive impact on where we are, and I learn so much from them. The loyalty my team has shown for our mission is extraordinary. My first team member is still with me today and our staff retention is close to 100 per cent. This is a KPI for our business, as human capital is our most important resource.

Aimee's vision and competence

Aimee teaches us how a business can align its resources and capabilities with a clear purpose. She has developed an aligned business strategy that has enabled her to raise capital and secure partners. Perhaps the most interesting insight is how she has ensured her product is much more than just a thing to be sold.

Acknowledging her 'core' product is tampons, she understands that her 'actual' product is much more than that: trusted and pure sanitary products for women, identified by the TOM Organic brand, the organic certifications, the aligned distributors, as well as the packing and display.

But her 'augmented' product offers still more, and includes the trusted conversations, the education and the culture of the people in the business. This ensures she need not be competing on price, volume, or standardised product metrics. Her resources and capabilities help position her products far away from her large multinational competitor offerings. Her strategy has successfully aligned her resources and capabilities with her vision and purpose.

43

AS A BUSINESS WOMAN YOU'VE GOT TO CONSTANTLY EVOLVE YOURSELF, YOUR BUSINESS AND YOUR TEAM.

What learnings from Aimee Marks can I take into my business?

15

OWNER AND MANAGING DIRECTOR OF FORWARD THINKING DESIGN

Vanessa Cullen started freelancing as a graphic designer during university. Jump forward 16 years and now she is the owner of Forward Thinking Design, one of the most awarded interior design and project management studios in Australia. Her passion and tenacity has helped her turn her dream into a successful business, built on it's reputation in the industry.

In the core of my being I truly understand that you have to make the most of each and every moment. That comes from some truly traumatic experiences in my life. When I was two years old I was diagnosed with nephrotic syndrome, a kidney disease which can be fatal. I was lucky to survive, but I didn't start off life very well. Growing up there was a lot of problems in my family. My sister suffered a brain haemorrhage when she was 15 years old that left her disabled. During my HSC I had to care for my seven year old brother alone while my parents were caring for my sister in hospital. I ended up with clinical depression as a result of the whole experience, but I overcame that and got life back on track. Then I found out I had polycystic kidney disease (PKD) and endometriosis. In defiance, I have since gone on to represent Australia in triathlon and also started the fitness and healthy eating blog morethanpkd.com.

The challenges I have faced in my life help me to appreciate everything that I have. I have an ecstatic moment at some stage in each day. I try to seek out every last little bit of experience and joy in each moment, whether it is in business, my blog, training for triathlons or just life itself. That's what drives me in everything I do.

Finding my niche

My interior design and project management business Forward Thinking Design started by default. Around 2003, I was studying and there were opportunities coming up on the university job board for people to design business cards and I was just like, 'well, why not?' So I registered an ABN and I got started.

From there it grew organically, but it got really serious when I spent a few years out in the restaurant and retail interior architecture field. I didn't like the ethics of the companies I worked for. There was a lack of respect for other people's intellectual property rights, and interns and staff were being paid poorly. I knew that those conditions were not necessary. I figured that if I couldn't find the right company for me I should create my own.

I concentrated on sourcing enough of my own work, so eventually I could form a viable company. I set out to create a business from the ground up, completely self-funded. I paid myself from day one, I just didn't pay myself much. It was a non-negotiable that I would have a salary, because my parents weren't well off and no one else was going to fund me. I had to have a salary from the beginning, even if it was a really low one.

The choice to start my own business, rather than be employed by someone else, boiled down to being able to sleep at night knowing I was making my own decisions. I also just love the lifestyle. I like to have a lot of other things going on at any one time and being my own boss gives me that flexibility. The comparison between my salary and what I would have earned if I were employed used to make me cry to think about in those early days, but the choice to have my own business meant there were other things that I could have the freedom to do outside of work. That became something quite important to me, because it's more about being happy in life than being über-wealthy. For me, it's much more about satisfaction.

The business became a company in 2010, so it was seven years of hard work to get to that stage. In the first three years there were points where I thought, 'is this worth it?' My team and I were working in my parents' front room until we outgrew the space. It wasn't easy making the step to an office with the added stress of rent, but we did it. Today the business fluctuates between five and seven staff. We also subcontract other designers and have SEO people, accountants and legal advisors.

As an athlete, blogger, PKD Foundation of Australia ambassador, and business owner I've got more on my plate than ever before but I don't see it as difficult. Once you get to that point in your life where you're really happy, it's okay, despite the fact that you don't have a minute to waste. Every day is jam-packed full of fun; it doesn't feel like hard work because I love what I'm doing and I have a great support crew.

Surround yourself with great people

I have a really open policy with my work team and ask their opinions about everything. I'm no genius. I hire people who are good at the things I'm not good at, so I'd be stupid if I didn't ask them what they think and give them the opportunity to be entrepreneurs, too. It's a great office culture to be part of. I'm not as hands-on anymore. I'm in a management role and work in art direction, so if it wasn't for my team I wouldn't be able to juggle everything.

With each of my team members it was a matter of determining what motivates them, and writing their contracts and KPIs accordingly. Now they're clear on what they're expected to achieve and it's a process that has been undertaken in collaboration with them. In their quarterly reviews I always let them say what they think they've earned and that keeps them honest to themselves.

Building relationships is the key to my success

The way the business has grown has been entirely through word-of-mouth. With me, it's all face-to-face networking and that's how I've built relationships over the years. I'm the NSW junior vice-president of the Australian Shop and Office Fitting Industry Association, so I have a close relationship with most of the shop fitters in the industry, and that means they often sub-contract us. I've worked on developing referral relationships with a lot of people and that is our number one advantage by far. In our industry it takes a long time for you to earn your stripes and for you to earn those relationships.

My mentor is Ron Geekie, the owner of Oz Design Furniture and Amber Group. He has been an invaluable resource to the business. He has a wealth of experience and he just gets me, and he gets business. Being a retailer means he comes from my customer's point of view. My biggest weakness was a lack of business experience, so under his mentorship I have learnt a lot. You give him a problem and he's got a person who can help you find the solution.

I relied on Ron's expertise to help me improve our processes. The business was profitable, but it just wasn't doing what it should have been doing. We bill for time so we needed to accurately account for the time spent on projects. Ron, together with my uncle and father – both of whom come from finance backgrounds – all brought their experience to the table. I enlisted them to look objectively at the business to tell me what needed to be improved. I didn't really understand how much we needed to drill down on tracking our time until they came in and gave me their viewpoints.

We brought in Xero and WorkflowMax software to focus on efficiency. We chose the right software and the sailing has been smoother over the past two years since we went through that profit building process.

Setting my company apart

Forward Thinking Design is a company out there winning business awards and that makes us different because design companies are great at going broke. We understand the business side and we know that our clients do not have a never-ending pot of money. Customers know that we deliver on time and within budget. But this reputation can be a double-edged sword: sometimes we're not given the opportunity to work with big budgets because in people's minds we're the tight budget problem-solvers.

The things that differentiate us from the competition are that we do a lot of strategy work and we're known for focusing on client return on investment. Forward Thinking Design has a reputation for being able to produce incredible looking spaces on tight budgets, tight time frames and in challenging scenarios. We're quite a different design company, because we do a lot of initial research and business planning work with our clients. Often we'll be contracted by big brands to undertake analysis of their current retailing and reposition them in the market.

I don't cold pitch much anymore, because I've done so much qualification work trying to find the right contacts and a lot of our leads are brought in by referrals. We're lean in terms of that whole process. At the start of my business I didn't have pre-qualification down to a fine art, but now we're a lot more efficient in screening leads.

We're trying not to have a design style, because our work is not about us, it's about our clients. Every business that comes through our door is unique and our portfolio has to look unrecognisable as a particular firm. I think too many design firms end up with a trademark 'look' and I really hope we never do.

You've got to ask for help

If there were one piece of advice I would give my younger self it would be to get more advice from more experienced people earlier. Even if it costs you a lot of money that's the one thing I think you've really got to invest in when you're young.

I think the reason so many businesses fail is because people are great at what they do and not very good at business. Unless you really want to learn about business and you are really passionately interested in business strategy, then you shouldn't do it. I'm a creative person, but I like being creative with strategy and direction, and the bigger business picture. The challenges that most creative people find really boring and restrictive, I find really interesting and engaging, and that has allowed me to succeed.

Vanessa's vision and competence

How can any firm stand out in a crowded industry? Vanessa gives some strong advice in her vision – start with the customer and build unique competencies. Competencies are a firm's combinations of resources (things you have) and capabilities (what you do with those things). These can lead to competitive advantage if they are:

1. *Valuable* (clients recognise the worth of these integrated designs and are unable or unwilling to do it themselves).

2. *Inimitable* (if they can't be copied or it is too costly to copy them, perhaps because of trade secrets, legal protections, such as copyright or employment contracts, and so on).

3. *Rare* (for example, Forward Thinking Design's competence is hard to replicate as it takes many years of study and experience to build such abilities).

4. *Organisationally relevant* (the firm is organised to take advantage of these resources and capabilities – for example, through the advisory board, the workflow and accounting software, the know-how built in-house, and the strong referral networks).

These resources and capabilities have led to competitive advantage for Forward Thinking Design, and Vanessa is clear that an indicator of their success is the lack of recognisable watermark in the firm's portfolio of work: it can and should be all about the customer.

WE'RE GOOD AT BUSINESS. YES, WE CREATE BEAUTIFUL SPACES, BUT SO CAN EVERY DESIGN FIRM OUT THERE. WE FOCUS ON THE THING THAT WE'RE DOING DIFFERENTLY AND THAT'S END TO END RETAIL STRATEGY.

ERIKA GERAERTS

CO-FOUNDER AND DIRECTOR OF WILLOW & BLAKE AND FRANK BODY

Photographer: Brooke Holm

Erika Geraerts doesn't call herself an entrepreneur. She just has a business or three. Willow & Blake was an idea that Erika and her two friends Bree and Jess, dreamed up as an online passion project to house their writing. The online publication transformed into a content and social media agency where these friends used their writing skills to help brands tell amazing stories. They now have a caffeinated skincare range called frank body that allows the women to put their social media marketing skills into action for their own brand. frank body continues to grow and is now being sold around the world.

When I was at high school I decided I wanted to pursue writing. I've always loved it and been interested in people and their stories. I assumed that I'd probably move to Sydney and work my way through all the magazines, because at the time those were kind of the only options that we were presented with.

While I was studying journalism at university I entered a competition with my friends Jess and Bree. The prize was a website build and we were all writing in our spare time and had our own blogs. We wanted to create an online publication. We submitted our entry, a 25 words or less statement, on a marketing agency's Facebook page. I ended up getting my first full-time job from that entry, because the managing director of the agency liked my writing style and they wanted to apply that to their own social media.

I worked with that agency for two years and I learned so much. I had an inspiring boss who saw the important role social media was going to play for marketing. After almost two years I felt like I had learnt all I could in that position. My role had gone across to account management and social copywriting, and it was a bit more spread out than I wanted it to be. I wanted to focus solely on writing.

At the same time Bree and Jess were working in their respective fields as well, in PR and journalism. We all had that itch to do our own thing, and knew there was an idea behind that competition entry in the online publication we had dreamed up. We were writing blogs on various things, like food, fashion and music, and we thought that's what this online publication would be about. After a bit of research we realised it was a saturated market. We turned our focus on to the people behind the things we loved and started writing profiles.

Willow & Blake was born

When we launched Willow & Blake it was an online profile editorial publication. We wanted to write profiles about the people in the areas we loved, that gave a glimpse of who they are beyond the brands or businesses that people already know.

We started writing these profile pieces and paired them with beautiful photography that tied into the brand image we created for the website. The website was running while we were working in our jobs.

Six months in we thought we could actually turn it into a business, because we started getting a lot of freelance writing requests off the back of it. Jess and I were the first to leave our full-time positions. We turned Willow & Blake into the business site, offering copywriting and social media for clients. Bree joined us a year later.

Bree, Jess and I were quite realistic at the start with Willow & Blake. Even my Mum had said to me that most businesses fail in their first year. We were willing to work hard at it and would do work for free or for low rates to try and get our name out there. It required a lot of patience. If it's what you believe in and love, you just persist. You really have to love the business that you're in, because when it's not paying enough that love supports you and drives you to keep going.

Four years down the track we have a team of six. We have also developed our own brand and product, frank body. We had so much experience with online branding, tone of voice and social media development and we wanted to use that for ourselves. We came up with a coffee body scrub, which has been a crazy success.

Our social background helped frank body flourish

frank body developed because we saw a gap in the beauty market, and we felt like a lot of the existing beauty brands were disconnected from their audiences. We wanted to create a product where we could have full control and not be limited by clients' expectations. We have two other business partners in frank body: Alex, and Steve who owns a few cafés in Melbourne. Steve had women coming to him and asking for coffee grinds to use as a body scrub. That piqued his interest and he talked to his partner Bree about it.

They went and did a little bit of research and saw that coffee scrubs are a do-it-your-self recipe online, but no one was packaging, marketing and selling it. In the beginning we were making that product ourselves by hand, so we could dictate the supply by the demand. We knew we could develop an engaging, fun brand that targeted the 18 to 24-year-old girl who was making purchase decisions through Instagram and online retail.

The idea behind the voice of frank body developed quickly. We were trying to build a brand identity on social media, but it was also about educating consumers about the benefits of coffee scrubs. The ingredients were really simple and written on the back of the pack, and it was quite inexpensive to make. We knew we couldn't dress it up and charge $80; we knew we had to be honest and keep it simple.

We had a light bulb moment where we just had to be 'frank' with our customers and direct about the nature of a beauty routine. That was the moment when everything fell into place, and we developed that hashtags #letsbefrank and #thefrankeffect, which now have over 100,000 tags online.

We had an aggressive social media strategy at the start. We were posting almost every hour on Instagram, sourcing as much content as possible and used a cheeky tone of voice that got people's attention.

One of the biggest parts of the frank body brand is for girls to identify with the character and start conversations with a phantasm on social media. The tone of voice and style we have used for frank allows our customers to be fun and playful, and removes the taboo associated with beauty routines.

At Willow & Blake we would take any client and try to develop a user-generated content strategy, so we applied that to frank. We tried to get customers to take on that ambassador role for a brand and spread the product by word-of-mouth. We're doing things a bit backwards now to other beauty brands. They are trying to get online and develop the social presence, while we're trying to develop an offline presence, whether that's through retail or traditional advertising.

We value our identity as a dot com business so much and it's been incredible to be able to have full control over the brand. The problem is not everyone engages online or on social media. Strengthening our offline presence would allow us to connect with a wider audience.

Our business has grown organically

Willow & Blake didn't have any capital investment. We were fortunate to win the competition to have our website built, so that saved us the cost of setting up the Willow & Blake site. It was hard and we were struggling for a while. The business was based on us building relationships with people and growing from one client to 30. We funded frank body ourselves and have used the success of the business to drive our expansion.

Initially, we were making the product in Steve's café. The boys were leading the product development while Bree, Jess and myself were working on the brand and the marketing. It started growing beyond our capabilities, so we spent a bit of time researching manufacturers in Melbourne.

We're led by our customers and what they want. We've done two surveys now and we've got some pretty amazing feedback on what they want the brand to be. We have another social account called @frankfeedback, which gathers results that people have been sending from using the products on several skin conditions, including eczema, psoriasis, acne and even stretch marks. The feedback has been incredible and prompted us to look into doing clinical trials and preparing our own studies on the effects of caffeine topically.

We find our staff through word-of-mouth

Willow & Blake started as us wanting to write about people, and we've tried to always hire people who share the same values as us or who we can call our friends, as well as one of our colleagues. I am constantly out and about, meeting new people and working with people who have great ideas. As long as I'm around people who I enjoy doing that with, I will try anything and I'm always up for a challenge.

We will have people come to Willow & Blake with a million ideas and it's one thing to talk about things, but another to go and do it. I have made a promise to myself that I'll never say I'm going to do something unless I actually intend to do it. Otherwise, you throw around ideas, and if you say something and don't accomplish it you internally let yourself down.

We've always had some sort of connection with the people we have hired so far. We are mainly looking for someone who has a knack for writing. Culture fit is also important for us. We're a small office of 15, so we want someone who is willing to learn, who will ask questions and can take on feedback. We see ourselves as one big family and we all sit down for lunch every second Thursday together. We've advertised a few times online for certain positions, but we've always come back to people who have been introduced to us or who connected with us through another contact.

Be patient with your business

Carefully choose who you partner with for your business. You should know their bad side and you should have had an argument with them beforehand, so you know how they argue or how you argue together. Find someone who has strengths that you don't have. There's no point having three people with the same skills. You want to be able to hold each other up when you can't hold yourself up.

Erika's tips for startups

When it comes to starting your own business have realistic expectations in the beginning that things take time. The four things I really value are patience, persistence, kindness and curiosity. Those are the main things I think business owners need to have to find happiness and success.

Erika's vision and competence

Willow & Blake gives some sound advice with regards to the building and strengthening of resources and capabilities. For many businesses, the key resource or capability is people. The challenge of hiring a new person to work in the team is significant. We know we should hire people with certain skills and experiences to complement the existing team. Entrepreneurs are increasingly realising that the best way to identify people is not by the traditional process which included advertising, requesting a polished CV, and interviewing shortlisted candidates.

Bree, Jess and Erika know that it's often the cultural fit that determines whether an employee will flourish, and that the key dimension of this manifests in behaviours: How do they react in a stressful situation? How do they interact with existing members of the team? These behavioural and habitual actions and reactions often give far better insight into the appropriateness of a potential employee. They can provide more valuable insight than a short interview or from sophisticated psychometric testing.

● **Notes**

7

MELANIE PERKINS

CO-FOUNDER AND CEO OF CANVA

Photographer: Christopher Morris

Melanie Perkins was a 19-year-old university student when she had the idea for her first business. She wanted to create a design tool that rivalled software produced by multinationals, but she wanted to make it simple, intuitive and, best of all, free. Canva has more than five million users who use to tool to create and communicate, and the business is valued at $165 million.

The Canva journey began back in 2007, while I was still studying at The University of Western Australia. I was teaching students how to use design programs, but they were struggling with the technical aspects of each program. I saw that the future of design was going to be online, collaborative and simple.

I wanted to put this concept into action and my co-founder, Cliff Obrecht, and I created an online yearbook design tool called Fusion Books. People loved the idea and now it's the largest yearbook provider in Australia. I was 19 at the time and deferred uni to focus on the business. I knew there was more to this idea than yearbooks and we opened the concept up to a full online design tool, now known as Canva.

We launched Canva in August, 2013. The vision for Canva is to empower everyone to create and communicate. We've grown to four million users and are a daily tool for many social media marketers, bloggers and small business owners. We have also launched Canva for Work with added features to allow businesses to create beautiful designs.

Technology has changed every single aspect of society; every single job, every single industry. We were lucky enough to see an opportunity and we jumped at it. Now we have a great team of designers, developers, artists, marketers, investors, and advisors. It's been an incredible journey so far and it's only the beginning.

You have to learn on the job

I like to call my process 'just-in-time learning'. I ask and learn about something when I need to know about it. For example, when we were learning about raising investment we spoke to as many people under the sun as we could and got their opinion. I completely fill my brain with every single resource I can, speak to every single person I can, and learn as much as I can about whatever it is. There's so much to learn so you can't possibly know everything up front. You do have to learn on the job. It always happens 'just in time'.

There have been so many things to learn and so many mistakes we have made along the way, but those things have been part of the journey. If you go straight to the finish line what would be the fun in that? When I first started, I had no business experience, product experience or marketing experience. I had to learn everything as I went. The most important thing has been the ability to learn.

Put your heart and soul into whatever it is you're doing, whether it's your schoolwork or a hobby. If you actually see yourself achieving things and you can set your mind to something that's the most important thing. It means you're measuring up to a challenge rather than thinking you can't do it. Eventually you will see yourself achieve and succeed many times over. If you believe you can do something and then you achieve it, then you can do the next thing that comes along.

Your idea should solve a problem

The most important thing for a startup is to solve a real problem. Find something that is truly significant. Find a problem faced by lots of people. With Canva, the problem was that creating engaging, professional looking graphic design was incredibly difficult unless you had expensive software and spent years studying. We stand out in this space because we are doing something completely different. Where products were complex to learn, we wanted to make ours easy. Where other products were intimidating, we wanted ours to be fun. Where products took years to learn, we wanted ours to take seconds. We want to empower the world to design.

My job is really challenging, but it's my absolute dream job. I get to work with the smartest people I know, they are passionate and motivated and such a pleasure to work with. Being an entrepreneur should be an option that people consider. What do you love? What makes you tick? Consider those things and then make the choice to go for it.

I've found support on this journey

My Mum has been an incredible supporter. Even little things, like when I was in primary school I'd get to imagine a theme for a party and be able to see that into fruition. I'd have this concept for a Halloween themed, fairy-light lit birthday party and then I would do it. I got to see my vision become a reality.

That taught me to think big and believe in what is possible, rather than being bound to what already exists. I've learned to get the most out of opportunities, because I dream a little bigger, and having the support of my Mum the whole way has been a strong enabler for me.

When I came up with the concept of Canva I believed in it so much and had a vision of what it could become. I am very lucky to have two amazing, supportive and awesome co-founders, Cliff and Cameron Adams. When Cliff and I set out to raise funds, we made hundreds of revisions to our pitch deck. It took a year to get it to a point where people could see my vision the way I wanted them to. Now we have raised more than $12.6 million from investors that it has allowed us to expand so rapidly and create this tool that is free for users all over the world. Our investors have helped to open so many doors.

Setting goals can help you grow

It's really important to set goals. Set a goal such as making $100, it doesn't particularly matter how you make the $100, you could make something and then try and sell it, you could try tutoring a school subject. Setting a little goal like this and then being able to achieve it will teach you so many important lessons.

When I was 14 years old I had my first small business. I made scarves and sold them to five women's boutiques around my area in Perth. That opened up a whole new world to me, because I could create something that I could sell and make a profit.

No matter what the goal is, when you achieve it your self-belief will grow. From there you can move on to do bigger business. Actually going and making your first $100 is one of the most important things you can do to just give yourself that self-belief. Doubting yourself is so debilitating and restraining. As soon as you can change that, you can start to do anything.

Failure is a part of entrepreneurship

There was a moment before I took on any venture capital that I realised that there were only two options if we took this money. One was success and the other was failing to the point where we couldn't pay that money back. If we failed it would be extremely difficult and it could take the rest of my life to recover from it. At that point I had to decide that failure was a part of the process of entrepreneurship. There is the possibility that when you start a company and you take on funding that you might fail.

One of my investors, Lars Rasmussen, was co-founder of the wildly successful project Google Maps and also Google Wave, an ambitious project that didn't go the way he was hoping. That had a significant toll on him and it was a really challenging time. He realised that it had always been a potential outcome and was able to deal with it. That was a big, important decision I had to make early on. You can try and try and try, and I'm absolutely that way inclined. I'll try first as long as it takes, but at some point, regardless of how hard you try it might not work. As an entrepreneur, I do everything I can to avoid failure, but it's important to remember that it's part of the game and you'll learn so much from the process.

Melanie's vision and competence

Melanie's advice to find a significant problem faced by many people can also be wrapped into the important aspects of learning. She understands her business strategy is about being different, and she is deliberately choosing a set of activities that will create value.

From Canva, we see that one of its core capabilities is to be market-led (the ability to develop products meeting the needs of people wanting engaging professional-looking graphic design that is simple to do and low cost). It does not follow a product-led innovation (for example, discovering a new molecule and then finding ways for this to be used by someone or designing a new app and then finding how people use it).

Successful entrepreneurs oscillate between these two extremes, and ensure that they prioritise neither. The resulting learning is essential for the business as much as for the entrepreneur. Melanie understands her business strategy is about being different, and she is deliberately choosing a set of activities and products that will create value. The inspiration for this difference comes from her understanding people's problems, and that can be an extremely valuable competence.

THERE HAVE BEEN SO MANY THINGS TO LEARN, AND THERE HAVE BEEN SO MANY MISTAKES TO MAKE, BUT THOSE THINGS HAVE BEEN PART OF THE JOURNEY.

IF YOU GO STRAIGHT TO THE FINISH LINE, WHAT WOULD BE THE FUN IN THAT?

Melanie's tip for startups

The most important thing for a startup is to solve a real problem. Find something that is truly significant. Find a problem faced by lots of people. With Canva, the problem was that creating engaging, professional looking graphic design was incredibly difficult unless you had expensive software and spent years studying. We stand out in this space because we are doing something completely different. We are disrupting the design industry.

BIANCA KRISTALLIS

FOUNDER AND CEO OF PAMPER HAMPER GIFTS

Bianca Kristallis was a 26-year-old stay-at-home mum of young twins when she launched her luxury online hamper company as a hobby in 2004. Fast forward to 2015, and Pamper Hamper Gifts is turning 11 years old. Bianca says the key to her success and the reason why she has been able to turn her passion into profit comes down to her sheer determination.

From a young age I was gifted with work ethic. I think that's because every time I asked my Dad if I could have some money, he would say 'no'. By the time I was 14 years old, I was determined to buy myself some Reebok sneakers and to show Dad I was independent and determined to succeed, so one day I went to the mall and came back with a job at Sportsgirl. His 'no' made me hungry for financial success.

I started my online hamper business, because I wanted to be a stay-at-home mum who had flexibility and a stable income stream for my family. I financed $30,000 on my home mortgage and that enabled me to build a dynamic e-commerce website, invest in critical stock, and get my logo and advertising paraphernalia ready. This was all before businesses understood the benefit of online retailing.

No one really talks about investing most of your money in a kick-ass website and it kind of annoys me, especially if you have an online store that's integral to your business's success. If you don't have a high-end, sophisticated website that works brilliantly, there's no point being online.

A lot of startups try to save money by using template websites and generic images, but no matter what you do – no matter what industry you're in – if you don't invest in a quality website from the start this will reflect on your business brand. So in a nutshell I have learnt you need to speculate to accumulate. If customers can't navigate the site or integral information on the company, brand and ethos they will not trust your offering and will seek another provider. This is really important.

My little hobby had to work

I didn't expect my company to be a full-time all-consuming operation, but my idea fell into place and ended up taking over my life, and I became the breadwinner of my family. My little hobby was working, it was now real and happening, and I had to give it a go and make it happen. I owed it to myself and my children to make it a success.

People told me along the way I couldn't achieve certain things: 'are you crazy?', 'are you serious?', 'really?', 'online?', 'that's risky'. I used to hear all those negative phrases from family and friends, and people around me. Support, recognition and praise only came after I began winning awards: 'oh right, she has actually made something of this. We'd better back down now'.

My lightbulb moment was when I realised I had two little mouths to feed, then this business had to work. Before I knew it, I landed a large corporate order and that got the ball rolling.

Apparently, my first Pamper Hamper Gifts customer was an online competitor who knew a young mum was about to start a hamper company and she could potentially become serious competition. A staff member ordered a hamper to their home, then took it to their Monday morning meeting where it was critiqued. They laughed and mocked the business concept, and the fact that we used black tissue paper. Now everybody's using black tissue paper.

In year two of my business I nearly sold it, because it just wasn't making any profit, and I was caught up in being a mum – breast-feeding, trying to raise my twins, trying to deal with an unsupportive husband.

A few weeks before the buyer signed on the dotted line one of the big banks placed a really large order that was critical to the business's cash flow and this enabled me to reinvest the money back into the company. By the end of year four, which was when my marriage broke down, I had a business that was actually starting to make a profit. I was feeling positive. I said to myself, 'I need to pick myself up here. This has to work, it's going to work; it's looking good and things are great. I'm one of the only luxury hamper companies in the market. Keep going, Bianca'. And I did.

I felt there was a need in the market for luxury gifting in a box at an affordable price. I believed Australians needed to be educated that baskets, curling bows, raffia and cellophane were long gone; that you can spend $100 and create a classy, elegant gift that comes in a beautiful box that you can up-cycle and keep.

I love networking – it's the key to my success

I've always been a people person and I knew that to get the brand out there I needed to network, so I started entering various Australian business competitions. For example, I entered the Australian National Business Championships in 2010 and 2012, and we won the national prize for Best Small Online Business both years.

Then I entered the Telstra Women's Business Awards in 2011, and was a finalist in the marie claire Young Business Women's Award category, which was fantastic. I soon realised that getting your name out there and becoming friends with other business women – or even men who have the same mindset, skills and abilities as you – really helps. This also places a face behind the brand, giving confidence to potential customers.

A lot of my database has been achieved through networking, sticking by friends that I've made along the way, and keeping the connections going. Networking is definitely the reason I've got this far. I've also really thought outside the box. Each time a competitor comes into the marketplace it makes me stronger and more determined. It makes me want to do the opposite of what they're doing. I don't like being copied and the minute that happens I disrupt and change it up.

I generally come up with my ideas for the year ahead of time, in January, when I'm lying on a deck chair on Hamilton Island with the twins. The ideas generally come into play by mid-year. As I'm proactive in my planning, I keep ahead of the competition by having that next idea ready to go, so the minute someone tries to do something the same, I unleash what I've had hidden for a few months. I'm highly creative, so being original and authentic is what I want to be known for in my industry.

I'm really proud of my packaging. It took about five years to get the shape, height and colour right. If you're having packaging made, think about shipping – you don't want to be paying to ship air. I developed a box that can be flat-packed and the amount of time that went into achieving that was unbelievable. I look at my boxes now like they're my little babies. They are part of Pamper Hamper Gifts – they're iconic.

I love what I do, every day is different and challenging. Because a lot of competitors are coming into the marketplace – every day we are seeing them on social media – it keeps me on my toes. It's healthy; I don't mind seeing it. I'm never one to give up. I soldier on.

Delegating is a fine art

I can pretty much run my business sitting on my laptop in a café, spending my whole day delegating. We don't rely on our location; we can operate from the bottom of Ayers Rock. Delegating is something I've always been good at. It's much easier just being able to flick an email to my SEO guy saying, 'do this, do that', and flick an email to my accountant, publicist or web developer.

I outsource all of my SEO and SEM marketing, as well as accounting, photo editing and packaging. We do all our own photography in-house, and then we send the images to specialists who tweak and enhance them. I'm actually one of the photographers; I have developed a real love for it, too.

I only hire casuals, so if we come into a quiet patch, I'm not committed to paying a lot of wages. It just makes business sense to have casual workers in my set up.

Every day there are four of us in the office. I've got pickers and packers – they make hampers and help me with photoshoots, styling and photography. Then I've got another girl who helps with quoting, new business and sending out gifts to the charities and causes that we support.

Everybody who works for me tends to do everything that I do. I like to teach everybody what I do, so if I'm ever stuck or in a turmoil somebody can pick up where I left off. There are no secrets, everything is shared. There's no specific roles for every single person working here. Everything is kind of the same, because I outsource a lot of the hard bits. At Christmas, there's up to 15 people working at any one time. We begin to get the large corporate Christmas orders from around October. Being prepared and organised with stock, staff and packaging is what we strive for at this time of year.

Managing stock is really hard

After 11 years of running this business I know how much stock to have on hand. It's about not over-ordering, not over-capitalising and ordering when the client needs the stock. So everything you see on the website is in stock to a certain level. If someone places an order and they need more, we have fantastic client relationships to ensure we can fulfill these orders. I would say we've got 10 of each item in the office. If someone places an order and they need 20 or 30, we just ring our wholesalers and order more, and fill the order.

We have now developed a stock system that works for our business. It took about five years to get that process right. It's really hard. If you don't perfect stock ordering it can jeopardise your business.

In the first two years we were holding a lot of stock and I was concerned about the viability of the business. I had ordered some products that weren't right for my target market, but I found a way to divest it on other websites and at some of Sydney's markets.

It took a little time to get to know my customer and to know who I was targeting. I went into business wanting to target the high end of the market – the corporate – but once I realised it was the EAs and PAs who were buying from us, then I listened to them and tried to understand what they liked. Expos are great for this. Every year we aim to exhibit at certain trade shows and meet our customers face-to-face. This enables us to ask them questions about what products and brands they wish to see in the hampers.

Working with what you've got

My business makes a profit, which is something I have strived to achieve. I work with what I've got and I'm a fan of reinvesting profits to assist with growth and expansion. Over the years I made a choice to grow my business slowly, because I didn't want to saturate the market and have people say, 'oh, there's Pamper Hamper Gifts again, how boring'. I've gone out into the marketplace in small increments. I think I can probably go a little bit faster now and expand a bit more.

My buzzword is longevity. I don't think there's enough support in the media and enough talk about businesses that have been there for a gazillion years and are still thriving. Don't get me wrong, I love 'startups', it means Australians are becoming more savvy and are helping transform our economy and create jobs of the future. I especially love mentoring the next generation of online entrepreneurs, however leaving a legacy is important. I'm still going and failure hasn't come into my picture yet.

Bianca's tip for nailing your logo

I wasted a lot of time getting my logo right from the start. I didn't interview enough graphic designers, I rushed it and overpaid for the work. I suggest going to about three or four different graphic designers and asking them to mock up about 10 different ideas each. A logo is so important, because if it's not right it can jeopardise your branding. It's one of the first foundations of your business brand.

Bianca's market

Among the many lessons that Bianca shares, one that stands out is her ability to keep ahead of her many competitors by continually innovating to exceed her customers' expectations. She has redefined a product/service category, and realises the buyer of the product is not necessarily the user of the product.

She ensures the entire shopping experience (from online selection, to presentation, to delivery) is unique and exceptional. Pamper Hamper Gifts shows that successful entrepreneurs need to master how to sell it, as well as what to sell.

Things I have learnt from Bianca

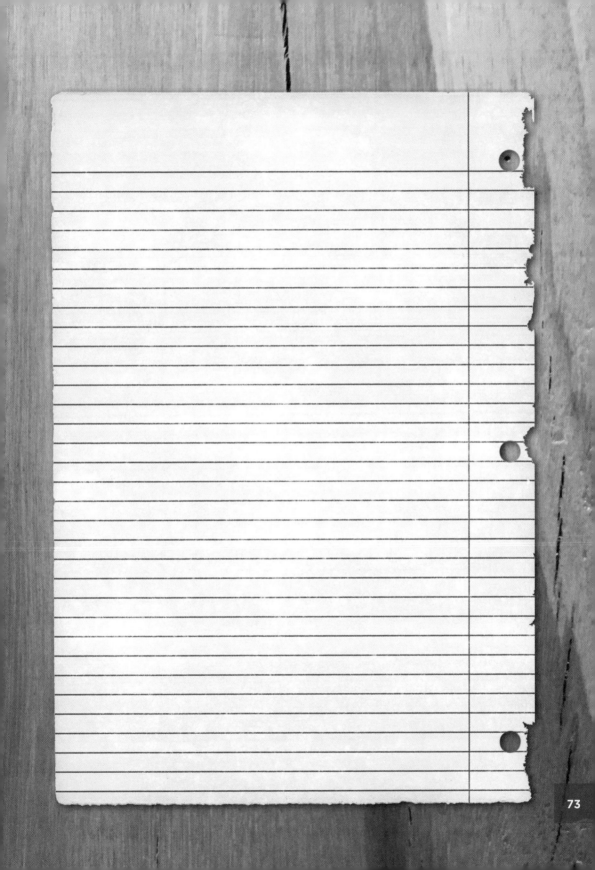

JANE LU

FOUNDER AND CEO OF SHOWPO

Showpo founder Jane Lu explains how she started her online retail business with no money and 'felt like a bum' working on her laptop on the sofa in her boyfriend's apartment. Now the business turns over more than $10 million a year.

I remember this moment vividly. It was around lunchtime and I was sitting at work doing my boring job, looking at my phone. Three hours had passed and all I had done was remove the circular referencing from my spreadsheet. I was thinking, 'this is so shit. I don't want to spend the rest of my life trapped in this cubicle. I need to get out'.

At the time, my business partner had been hassling me to quit my job, which I did, but then a month later she decided to fold the business. I was left without a job and without any other options. Because it was the GFC, I couldn't ask for my job back and it wasn't worth trying to get another one, so I just had to keep going, which is how I started Showpo.

Being in business with someone is almost like being in a relationship – you overlook your differences in opinion. None of my business partners have worked out. At the start you're so excited that you don't see how it might not work.

You can start a business with nothing

When Showpo started it was just online at first. I was sitting on the couch, not wearing pants, working on my laptop in my boyfriend's tiny apartment. I felt like a bum. I was still quite content with living off two-minute noodles and cask wine.

I didn't need to fund my start. You can start a business with nothing. I found another business partner and a wholesaler who gave me stuff on consignment, so I didn't need to pay for the stock until it sold. I filled the orders by myself, postage was paid for after we made the sale, I built the website by myself by googling HTML codes, social media was free and we gave the models clothes for the shoots. We did everything for nothing.

We spread the word through social media and we made up to $22,000 a month after just six months, which is pretty good considering at most we've probably spent $1,000 on Facebook ads to get that and the website I built was very amateur.

Three months after starting the online store (in November, 2010), we opened our first bricks-and-mortar store. It was a great sense of accomplishment, but I had to work in the store seven days a week. I would replenish stock by visiting suppliers in the morning, spent all my time serving customers in store and packing online orders during the day, and then at night I would work on the marketing – on social media. On the few days where we called a casual into the store, I could finally find time to squeeze in photoshoots. It was really hectic!

Then it got to the point where my business partner and I realised that we had differences in opinions on where we wanted the business to go and how we wanted to get there. We decided to amicably go our own ways. It was December, 2011, and despite it being the busiest month in retail, our online sales had shrunk down to 57 orders for the month. When I took over the business by myself, I surprised myself with the ability to work my butt off even harder, and from there sales literally doubled month-on-month. Now we're doing more than 500 orders a day!

Then we started hiring casual retail staff and caught one girl stealing from us. At first this made me weary about how much I could trust people, but then I realised it's all about finding the right people in the first place. I don't want to micromanage people. I've always favoured a really flat structure. I don't want to exert control over anyone and having everyone on the same level develops trust.

When you trust people, they appreciate that level of trust and work harder to prove their worth. And if everyone enjoys what they're doing and if everyone works well as a team, that makes the company culture great.

Even today hiring people is a constant struggle. Some people may look great on their CV, but you've got to find the right cultural fit. Then some people have the right fit, but even if they are motivated and want to learn, may not have the level of intelligence and skills for the role. When we interview people, they have to pass the 'airport test', which is, 'am I prepared to be stuck in an airport with this person if there's a delay?'

They also need to have the right attitude, because this is a small business. If someone doesn't do something, then I'll have to do it. For example, we asked a staff member to do an admin job and she was like, 'ugh, can't the intern do it?' If you work for a startup, you have to understand, no job is too small or beneath you.

Once you have a company culture, it makes a huge difference. Now, we sit around the family dining table at work and have lunch together and chit-chat over sandwiches and drinks. When you hire people you don't say, 'okay, we must have fun'. It happens organically.

Social helps you grow your customer base

We mostly use Instagram and Facebook to get the word out about what we're up to. Social's great because you get instant verification from your followers just from the number of likes and comments. You can test and trial, and if you're testing it by yourself you can react quickly. But you should always test, rather than just assuming your audience will have the same opinion as you.

Social media is also the best way to grow your customer base organically. It's not a hardsell, you grow your community by offering content that they want.

If you're an online retail startup, you've also got to have the right buying team. I have nine on my team, including myself. We've got two creative designers, two people in customer services, three in buying, and two in operations.

Marketing and social media is my passion. I can't live without my mobile phone. I've even tried watching YouTube while I'm showering, but it doesn't work. My phone feels like work now though. I can enjoy not having it around, but only if I'm entertained. If I'm just sitting there waiting for something, then of course I need my phone. But if I'm with friends, I can be without it. If I'm watching TV, I can be without it. TV's my other passion.

I think it would be great to outsource less, but there are definitely perks to outsourcing jobs. Our advertising is outsourced. We do our own organic social media, but our Facebook ads, Google ads and TV ads are all outsourced to agencies. Our warehousing is also outsourced and we've got a few virtual assistants to help. They deal with some of the admin and the easy customer service stuff. Our photographer is a contractor.

My purpose

When I first started Showpo, my purpose was to not go back to my corporate job and to prove myself. That was it for a while. Then I wanted to grow the business and challenge myself to see where I could take it. Now my purpose is just to have a vision with my team and to build them into something really huge.

An Australian-grown fashion company can have influence, and I want to build my reputation as a CEO, so I can make more of a difference to people's lives. One of my long-term goals is to open our own factories, have great work conditions and set the industry benchmark for how offshore factory workers should be treated. At the moment we sponsor Project Futures, which is the charity that aims to stop global human trafficking and slavery. There are also other things that I want to get involved in as the business grows and I have more freedom and time to do more.

You've got to be tenacious

There has been a lot of luck and the timing involved in what I've achieved. To be successful though, you've probably got to have the tenacity to keep going. When I look back and think about the times that I've struggled – it just seemed so bleak, but I just kept going. Maybe I was in denial, I don't know. I just thought 'oh, just keep going, it'll be fine'.

It took me two years to tell my parents I had quit my corporate job. They thought I was on extended unpaid leave from my job. I told them what I was really doing on Father's Day, 2012. I was like, 'so you know, I actually quit my job in July'. And they thought I meant the year before, in 2011. And I said, 'no, no, 2010'.

They couldn't believe it. They wanted to know how I had the guts to do it. They thought of themselves as being quite risk adverse – my Mum works in a bank and my Dad is an engineer. But I told them that they risked way more than me, when they immigrated to Australia from China in 1994, leaving everything. I think they have that risk-taking side to them, too.

Jane's tips for startups

• **You need to be obsessed with social media. This is not a task you can palm off to an intern. You need to get it, and in order to get it you need to be obsessed with it.**

• **Build your tribe. You need to find the right people to help you grow your business. Always follow your gut when you're interviewing.**

• **Don't be a perfectionist. You learn so much more from doing and making mistakes than you do from over-planning and wasting too much time on tweaking. Your idea of perfection is probably wrong in fact, and you won't know until you put it to market.**

Jane's market

Showpo demonstrates how social media can be used to both reach a customer as well as understand them. Jane's business is nimble because it is engaged with its customers as well as the broader industry and market trends. Showpo listens as well as broadcasts through social media – something that allows it to escape the 'me too' and price-driven acts of her competitors.

This 'conversation' is essential in a fashion-based business and shows how her alertness, tests and trials, and action underwrites the dynamism of a business. She also uses the 'ask, try, do, reflect' framework, which is a fundamental pattern by which entrepreneurs learn. Jane clearly understands the differences between data (likes and posts), insights (trends and fashions) and the framing of her opportunities (new lines and products).

NOTES

10

GABY HOWARD

CO-FOUNDER AND CEO OF THE PHOTO DINER

Gaby Howard set out to solve a problem in her own PR agency, but ended up creating a visual workflow solution for the fashion, interiors and beauty industries. She describes how building The Photo Diner was a daunting experience but now, three years and a re-brand later, she has her eye firmly set on the global market.

I didn't think of myself as entrepreneurial for a long time. From a young age I was given lots of opportunities and was told that I could do whatever I set my mind to. I went to a high school where you had to drive yourself to succeed. That set a really good theme for how I would work and how I saw my role in the workplace.

After studying and working in PR, I trained as a teacher, but wanted to give myself the opportunity to direct things myself. I started my own PR consultancy in 2010, which predominantly focused on fashion, lifestyle, entertainment and the not-for-profit industries. I had a lot of client images that I needed to distribute on a regular basis – but not just distribute, also store and relocate. And at the time, the only way to distribute those photos was by email, CD or USB stick, and it was really cumbersome.

I met my co-founder Nadine Cohen, who was a journalist for fashion and lifestyle magazines. We talked about the problem and she said that, as a journalist, it was hard to source photos for her stories. If she wanted an image of a black dress, she had to email an unmanageable number of brands and publicists asking if they had one. Then the emails would go back of forth. There was no transparency or editorial control over what was available.

I was planning to build some sort of solution for myself, but we then decided we would build a solution that helped the entire industry. That's how The Photo Diner came about. We launched in November, 2012, and focused on fashion in the first year, then we moved into interiors and beauty.

We realised we needed a technical co-founder

We self-funded our start and put in an equal sum of money. Then we quickly discovered we needed a technical partner, so we went through the process of trying to find someone. A lot of people told us that without a technical partner we would never receive any funding. So we were really stressed pretty early on. We had a great idea, but didn't know how to get it off the ground, because we couldn't find the right person to build it.

Fortunately, Nadine and I went to school with someone whose mum and her partner could help us. We reached out to Ruby Blessing and Nicholas McCutcheon and asked for support to get our idea to a point where it was ready to be scoped and developers could quote for the job. They fell in love with the project and said that rather than just helping us, they'd like to be part of it. They came on board as co-founders and as our design and tech team. Up until then, we had been really wary of having a platform developed that we had no control over and would have to continually add elements to it at huge expense.

We're a small team, so we do a lot of stuff ourselves and bring in consultants as we need them. We've had to be really selective with the people we have been able to bring on full-time. People often ask, 'how do you get such amazing people in the business?' It's been luck and we also sounded out people before we hired them. I meet people and I get a sense of whether they could work for us. Often I say, 'as soon as I can I'm going to hire you'. And they get really excited by the idea.

Having a great founding team has put us in a great position. It meant we could build an amazing platform for not a lot of financial outlay.

It was pretty daunting building it. We often felt we were in over our heads, but we tried to speak to a cross section of the industry to understand if this was something people wanted. Everyone was overwhelmingly positive and supportive. It took a lot of time and energy to get beyond that before people would really say what they needed from the technology. Then it was a matter of us having the confidence in ourselves to say, 'okay, so there's a lot of great feedback here and a lot of contradictions. What is smart advice to listen to and act on?'

At first we weren't confident enough to see that some pieces of information or advice could be left at the door. Really, the change only came when we realised that we needed to trust ourselves and believe in our own opinions.

Initially, we were uploading images ourselves, one by one while Nicholas built a multi-photo uploader. A lot of what we've done has been organic. People talk about agile development and that's really been how we've evolved. We've done as much consultation as possible, but not over-consulted either. Lots of clients ask for extra features, but it's about understanding where their request sits on our development pipeline.

We want to always do better for our clients. I'm really conscious of the fact that we're a platform that sells itself on making life easier, so there's pressure to make sure the functionality we're offering does that. One photo upload at a time doesn't quite cut the mustard.

We had to sell a concept before we could sell the product

I'm sure we could have done more market research, but we felt confident that we'd done enough. We were essentially creating a two-side business model and we had to create a business out of nothing. When we went to sell to fashion brands we had to show them PDFs of what it was going to look like. It was such a different concept and a different way of doing things that it was really challenging to explain it at first. It wasn't like creating a social network and saying, 'right, so we've got the concept straight, let's look at the functionality'. We had to sell the concept first.

The biggest challenge with pitching is keeping it super simple. We used to go in and say, 'we can do anything and this is everything we have. Look at all these buttons'. We got so excited about the cool things we had built and people just said, 'wow, that's great, but I'm not going walk away with any of that'. We simplified the message and now we say, 'here are three things that I'll talk to you about today'. If people walk away from the meeting remembering one thing, that's amazing.

In terms of clients, we have three types – small brands, established brands and PR agencies. Small brands are doing everything themselves in their business and don't feel supported in a lot of areas. They look at us as a low cost solution to a PR agency and we help them spread the word about their business. They feel they're supported with resources and they've got someone to talk to if they have any questions. The next level up from that is bigger, more established brands. They've got lots of employees and bigger budgets, and they want to maximise their time. PR is still a hard aspect of business to fund and it's always the first thing to go when times get tight. Generally, they've got lots of images which, in the past, literally sat on their desktop but now, with something like The Photo Diner, they can upload them all and make them available to the media. They're saving time and money by enabling their contacts to access everything from one location, and they have a platform that makes all their images accessible and available. It also gives them increased exposure across more of their imagery.

Our third type of client is PR agencies. Obviously, they have media contacts, are well established, and have money and resources. They want a tool that holds a number of images that they can work with on a daily basis. So again it's about functionality. They can access photo albums that help keep them organised and make all their images available to them. They receive the data about their photos, so they can see what's going on and who is downloading what images. And they can also use our platform to help manage their showroom inventory. It becomes more of an organisational tool for them.

Image licensing has never been a big problem for us, because we actually don't own the photos – the brand manages all their own photos – we just provide a platform to help increase the exposure. That was a decision we made early on, and it meant we could take a step back from all the issues around photo ownership.

To make sure brands felt safe about being on the site, we made it a closed platform, so you need to register before you can see anything, let alone have access to download anything. We also have a comprehensive permission system that sits across all the photos, so brands can have complete control over who sees and downloads their images.

We have big plans for the future

We found our first customers by speaking to people in our network. We asked stylists and editors we knew if they could make introductions. We used our first clients as sounding boards and we went back to them again and again. We have really strong relationships with them. We're constantly asking them, 'is this valuable, should we add that?'

We grew the business first through connections, then through word of mouth and client recommendations. We don't really do any advertising, we have social channels that we use to speak about ourselves and our clients.

We want our business to be the destination for media sourcing branded content globally. We might only be a tenth of the way there, but we do have an amazing platform and now we're focusing on how we get that out to more customers. We already have brands and agencies in the United States and the United Kingdom using it and we have had media from all over the world sourcing from the platform.

We've raised capital, but not much

Towards the end of last year we raised $450,000. We wanted to raise as little money as possible and instead use our own revenue to drive the growth of the business. It wasn't like we went out and got $5 million, and all of a sudden felt really comfortable and could hire loads of people. It still felt very much like we were under pressure – that we were still working on the business with a small budget.

The money has allowed us to build out the product a bit more. We had all these ideas for development, for adding functionality to the site and we also wanted to get our marketing message out there in a more efficient way. The money gave us the opportunity to start looking into that.

On the back of that raise, in late September, 2015, we re-branded and re-launched the site as Flaunter to coincide with some exciting product developments and the addition of video capabilities. This is an incredible period for the business and we're so excited about what we're delivering.

I was always in charge of the finances, but my financial literacy skills weren't at expert level. We were amazingly lucky early on, because a friend introduced us to our current corporate advisor, who's also now an investor. When you get to the investor stage, when you're talking about shareholdings and options, it can be daunting. She took a lot of pressure off us and enabled us to focus on the business while she helped to lead the investment round.

There is more pressure having investors on board, because there's other people's money in the business, but they don't put undue pressure on us. They obviously have different knowledge and skills they bring to the table, and connections. It has been a really positive experience.

I think the first few years are the hardest, because those years are all about your business finding itself. You don't necessarily know quite where you fit in yet. You don't necessarily have a business model that's concrete. Once you get past those early years it starts to feels more organised – a little less insane. Yes, the business is older and far more complex, but you feel more comfortable knowing there are these steps ahead that are pretty true for most companies. It's that first hill that's really hard.

You have to find the strength to keep going

Had we known everything we know now, we definitely would have thought twice before starting this business. To be honest, we had no idea what it meant to start a company of this size. I think that at times being naive really helps. You say to yourself, 'okay, I'm going to give it a go. I'm going to try my hardest. It's not the end of the world if it doesn't work, but how cool would it be if it did?'

It's important to be excited, but also true to yourself and know that not all businesses work. Also, you get out what you put in. It's never going to be easy and you do a lot of questioning. For people who have never had their own business before or started their own company, it's really important to understand that everything is on your shoulders and you get the best and the worst of that.

Gaby's tips for nailing it

• The most important thing is to really trust yourself. Mentors have been important in helping us learn to trust ourselves. Having someone to go back and forth with over an issue has been amazing, and more often than not I would get back to the same conclusion, but feel relieved that I'd had a sounding board. I know people say it a lot, but running a business can be isolating and you can feel like the weight of the world is on your shoulders. Having someone on your side with expert knowledge as a sounding board gives you that extra confidence when times are tough.

• Don't be afraid to ask people for things. I've asked so many people for favours and introductions over the past three years and everyone has been happy to help. Having warm introductions can massively affect your business. Make sure you're asking the right people for the right things though. Understand who you're targeting and make sure that what you ask of them is appropriate and brings value.

Gaby's market

Gaby gives us insight into the importance of seeing and understanding a business's different clusters of customers. All clients want a platform for managing images, but they have vastly different expectations of The Photo Diner and Flaunter's services.

One way to understand this is the activity of segmenting, targeting and positioning. This firstly involves segmenting markets (identifying, grouping and profiling clusters of customer needs). Gaby notes that the sophistication of the business, the expectation of services needed, and the budgets for solutions are different across the potential customer population.

The second step is targeting particular segments (evaluating the attractiveness of each segment and selecting those appropriate for your business). Note how The Photo Diner targets three segments: small brands, established brands and PR agencies. They know exactly what these clusters of customers want: whether this is a low-cost solution for a public relations firm, increasing exposure efficiently and effectively across diverse groups, or a sophisticated tool to manage images and provide insights into usage.

The third step is positioning the offering for those target segments (designing your product or service according to your customer's needs and wants). This signalling can include branding, packaging, functionality, usability, performance, but also pricing and service agreements or guarantees. Note that Gaby remains cautious, and that although the company consults with customers, they are careful about how they meet those customer expectations for features, and timing the required development pipeline. The final activity is developing a marketing plan for each target segment, ensuring the positioning is clearly communicated.

HAVING A GREAT FOUNDING TEAM HAS PUT US IN A GREAT POSITION.

IT MEANT WE COULD BUILD AN AMAZING PLATFORM FOR NOT A LOT OF FINANCIAL OUTLAY.

JESS AND STEF DADON

FOUNDERS OF HOW TWO LIVE

Three years ago, sisters Jess and Stef Dadon ran into an editor from Grazia magazine on the streets of Paris. The chance meeting helped launched their careers as social media influencers and inspired them to start their business How Two Live. Since then, they have worked with global brands, written a book, launched a shoe brand and accrued more than 118,000 followers on Instagram. Inspiring Rare Birds caught up with the pair in Los Angeles, where they were working for three months.

Jess

We started our daily blog in 2012. Stef was moving to Paris and we thought it would be a fun thing to do together while we were on opposite sides of the world from each other. Each day one of us would post what we were doing, where we were going and new wardrobe editions.

Stef

A few months into our blog we decided to go to Paris Fashion Week. I flew back to Australia for a wedding and while I was there we approached our favourite designers to dress us for fashion week. After a lot of 'nos', one PR company said 'yes' and we discovered they also represented lots of our favourite labels, so we had access to all these incredible outfits.

Jess

In a typical designer collection there are recurring prints or colours that fit together, so we chose outfits that we thought would photograph well together. At the time, the 'twinning' trend of dressing in matching outfits was really big, but it was a bit of a coincidence that we dressed like that.

Stef

Before we got to Paris, we emailed the designers and lots of them gave us tickets to their shows. One day, we were walking along the streets when this woman stopped us and said, 'oh my God, I love your outfits, can I take a photo of you guys?' She was Hannah Almassi, the fashion news and features editor at Grazia Magazine. She ended up doing a three-page article on the 'twinning' trend and we featured in it. The article was reprinted in several different countries, so that was pretty massive.

Jess

When the article came out, the number of people reading our blog and looking at our social media pages skyrocketed. A couple of months after that we started getting approached by brands. One of our first campaigns was for a label called Paint It Red. They hired us to style and model in their look book and campaign. The Paint It Red campaign received coverage in a bunch of magazines and we also did an in-store appearance, so it was an incredible opportunity.

We often get feedback that things we post on Instagram, or on our website, sell incredibly well. I think we've learned who our demographic is and what our reader likes. We make sure that anything we post fits in with our aesthetic and is something that our girl will love. That's what keeps brands coming back and wanting to work with us time and again. We really understand our followers and we make sure the brands we work with are a good fit, so that when they pay us for the service, we know they're going to see results.

We needed a manager

Stef

We were handling all the financial negotiations with brands for the first year and a half, and we loved it, but as we grew into a bigger company we realised we needed to find a manager.

A lot of what we do has a big focus on digital. Our managers are in Sydney and they have a great deal of experience in that area. We went through a couple of others first who weren't the right fit for us. A smaller agency really values us; they're out there every day trying to sell us.

Jess

We started our blog three years ago and over that time the industry has evolved. In the beginning a lot of brands would ask for things for free. It has taken time for the mentality to change and for brands to realise this is another place to put their marketing dollars. Now they see the value of working with influencers long-term and with real budgets, rather than just asking for a few free posts here and there.

Stef

How Two Live really taps into a demographic that a lot of brands struggle to hit, too. We speak the language, we know what they like, so we can offer brands a way to translate what they're doing into something that engages that younger girl.

Our intention has always been to grow organically. We could have started our store or our shoe label right off the bat, but we started by building an audience, which is the best way to do things nowadays.

Jess

And obviously there's no initial investment then.

Stef

Exactly, so in the beginning we had our own jobs and this was just something we were doing on the side. But we've built it into something where we can make money by working with these brands. We reinvest the money back into the business, and now have the resources to build our own label.

A lot of influencers work with brands and do one or two sponsored Instagram posts, whereas we like to build an ongoing relationship. For example, we recently worked with a brand on an Instagram takeover, wrote an article for its newsletter and did some nail art workshops. Rather than just working on one thing we target different platforms and work out a package of options. That leads to greater results for us and the brand.

Jess

Our girl is probably 14 to 20 years old and she loves to come and meet us and have photos with us. They love to get hands-on with whatever we're doing. We like to get up close and personal with our girl, and one way we do this is through workshops and events.

Stef

We focus on posting blogs on our website every day and we've written a book called *#HOWTWOLIVE*. That's been one of our main projects over the past year and we've also launched a shoe line called TWOOBS. We're pretty excited about it. It will run alongside How Two Live as a sister brand.

Jess

We see an opportunity here. What we do really speaks to the teenage girl and rather than saying, 'okay, let's be this one thing – let's be a blogger, let's be a store', we think, 'let's be everything to them'. We want to be their style inspiration and their big sisters. We want to give them advice and you can see that in the book, the shoes, the blog. We're expanding our website at the moment, so it's more than a daily diary. It will include style advice and general advice for teenage girls.

Stef

They'll also be able to shop a curated collection of whatever we're loving this week. And, as with everything we do, we're encouraging them to give back; whether it's through volunteering, donating money, or helping out a friend. We want to ensure we're helping to influence them in positive ways.

Jess

It's a teenage girl magazine, but the new-age online version that includes everything they could ever possibly want.

You have to get out there and meet people

Jess

Networking is huge for us. Being in LA is great, because there's an event every other night and even when you go out for dinner you'll meet someone at the next table. The other day we shared a table with a woman who ended up introducing us to someone at a big publishing company and now we're working with them. I think just being out there is important. Because there are two of us, and we do dress so crazily, we're a great walking, talking advertisement for our brand.

Before we came here, people told us that a lot of people in LA are all talk – that no one really follows through – so we were definitely wary of that. But this city is the Silicon Valley for digital influencers. The opportunities are 10 times bigger here than anywhere else in the world, but of course you have to work 10 times harder for them.

Stef

A lot of our followers are based in the US and California specifically. You really need to be in a place where your audience is to understand them, and we've hired a few interns while we've been here, so they'll be working on our collaborations with brands even when we leave. A lot of the people we work with are online. Our web designer is in the UK and our graphic designer is in Macedonia. We're using this new-age business model where everything is done globally.

We use a range of social media platforms

Jess

Our website is our core platform. We have quite a big Instagram following and on Facebook we have about 20,000 likes. We have quite a big following on Snapchat as well, because a lot of the younger age group is on Snapchat.

Stef

A year and a half ago we decided to focus most of our time on our social media. Our followers on Instagram were growing rapidly and that was where we were putting most of our content, rather than on our website. After speaking to a few people in the digital space we realised how important it is to keep your website as your main platform, as you never know what's going to happen to a social media platform or how it might change. So over the past six months or so we've been focusing more on our website and giving it the attention it needs. We've realised we can't have all of our eggs in one basket.

Jess

We're in the process of starting our own YouTube channel. Video is something we enjoy and we're slowly getting more into.

Stef

And Snapchat is one of the bigger up and coming platforms. It's about being real rather than planning things in advance and posting them when you're ready. And it isn't really about quality, which we love, because we can spend a lot of time editing photos for our website and worrying about whether things look good. Snapchat is a way for our followers to get up close and real with us. That younger age group is definitely looking for posts all the time, and they're constantly wondering what we're doing, so the platform works for us.

We look at our global metrics and often come up with a post schedule for Instagram based on that. But with the newer apps, like Snapchat, it's more about the constant stream of content.

Jess

Snapchat has been a big thing for us, because now we're really taking our followers with us on our journey through life. It's a constant reminder that people are watching and are interested, and excited about what you're doing. We feel more connected to our audience than ever.

A little 'no' won't stop us

Jess

Things grew organically for us from the beginning, and looking back we were pretty lucky. We were posting every day and we were definitely doing the right things instinctively, and then it became something we planned for. Now we come up with goals and plans and schedules, rather than just hoping for the best. I think a plan is crucial for success, but it's also about timing; we really just did get in with our blog at the right time. Now the market is a lot more saturated and it's a little harder to get noticed.

It's a really tough industry to be in. We're careful not to get too fixated with what has happened today, because often we can have a really tough day. But we have all these things in the works and we have goals that we're working towards. Obviously, there are always going to be setbacks, but having a plan keeps us on track and reminds us that we will get there eventually, despite a little 'no' today.

Having people around us who believe the business is incredible really helps. A fan will email us saying, 'I just wanted to let you guys know that you really inspire me'. Those are the things we remember and we'll be like, 'okay, this is why we're doing it'.

Stef

I think girls feel emotionally connected to us, because we don't care what other people think of us and we encourage others to do the same. That's why we really speak to that young girl, because if they've been bullied or feel like they don't fit in then they can turn to us for support. We give people the confidence to say, 'who cares? I'm going to wear what I want and be who I want be'. We've heard plenty of stories from people saying we gave them the confidence to be themselves, which is just so fantastic.

Jess

Our attitude shows in everything we do, and that's what people relate to. Anyone is welcome to join our little tribe of not caring.

Stef

We also know a lot of our readers are young, so as we mentioned we're constantly trying to be positive influences. In our book *#HOWTWOLIVE* we've written a section about How Two Make An Impact, and we talk through all the different ways they can help and give back. Thinking about fashion and looking good is great, but it's also important to have a greater purpose.

Jess

We didn't plan for this to become our full-time jobs or anything like that and we definitely had to work really hard to get it to where it is today. We were really lucky to meet Hannah Almassi in Paris, and all the other things that lead to such success. About six months into it we realised this was something we really wanted to do. We've had to pitch to brands and we've had more 'nos' than we'd care to count.

Even in LA at the moment, for every 'yes', we get 30 'nos' and it can be really tough. But working together as sisters makes it a little bit easier. We're not on our own, we have each other, and we know that if we keep working hard at it we'll keep seeing the results.

Jess's and Stef's content tips

The most important thing about content is consistency. For the first six months we posted on our blog every day at 10:00am. Even if you can't post every day, posting content regularly and consistently is important for building a readership.

We found that having a unique concept was what helped us stand apart from all the other blogs out there. For us, we played on the fact that we're sisters on the other side of the world writing an open diary to each other every day. Having that strong idea behind it definitely helped.

It's also important for us to understand what our readers want to read. Sometimes we'll post on Instagram saying, 'what do you guys want to see from us?' These days you can literally ask readers what they want, rather than guessing at it.

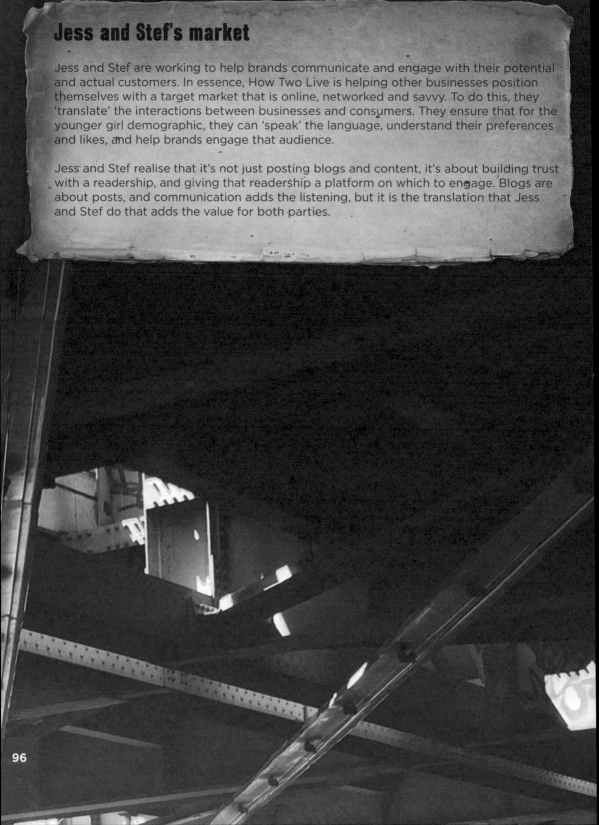

Jess and Stef's market

Jess and Stef are working to help brands communicate and engage with their potential and actual customers. In essence, How Two Live is helping other businesses position themselves with a target market that is online, networked and savvy. To do this, they 'translate' the interactions between businesses and consumers. They ensure that for the younger girl demographic, they can 'speak' the language, understand their preferences and likes, and help brands engage that audience.

Jess and Stef realise that it's not just posting blogs and content, it's about building trust with a readership, and giving that readership a platform on which to engage. Blogs are about posts, and communication adds the listening, but it is the translation that Jess and Stef do that adds the value for both parties.

Learnings from Jess and Stef Dadon

12.

LUCY THOMAS

CO-FOUNDER AND CEO OF PROJECT ROCKIT

ROSIE THOMAS

CO-FOUNDER AND CEO OF PROJECT ROCKIT

Back in 2006, Rosie and Lucy Thomas were two sisters fresh out of high school when they came up with the idea for PROJECT ROCKIT: Australia's youth-driven movement against (cyber)bullying, hate and prejudice. They wanted to tackle the issue of bullying in school and knew that it should be a conversation between young people. They didn't just set up a business; they started a social movement. Now the pair has developed an online version of the program, allowing every student and school in Australia to have access to cool, credible and in-touch anti-bullying development.

ROSIE

PROJECT ROCKIT was launched back in 2006 when Lucy and I were relatively fresh out of school ourselves. At the time, we never set out to create a movement, an organisation or to be a leading voice in cyber safety. We just saw a problem that needed fixing. We had an idea that we could fill a gap that wasn't being addressed, and that was the issue of bullying in schools.

Looking back, when it comes to my own experiences with the issue of bullying, I can admit that there were times when I was part of the problem and also times when I was part of the solution. However, it wasn't a singular traumatic experience that led me to want to set up PROJECT ROCKIT, it was more that I saw the impact that bullying had on many of my peers. I saw the way that being mistreated robs people of opportunities and smothers their development. This meant they learnt to hide the person they were or stopped putting their hand up in class. I thought this was incredibly unfair, and totally preventable.

We wanted to do something about this problem so we built a model of sending relatable young people into schools to run interactive workshops. We didn't preach, lecture or judge, instead we used real talk to inspire real change in young students.

LUCY

We started lobbying to get ourselves into schools to run these workshops. At first the challenge was convincing teachers who were a generation older than us that two young girls had value to add. We had to prove that this education should be delivered by young people and not by teachers, and that they should pay us to do it.

At the time we started PROJECT ROCKIT social media wasn't prevalent. Facebook had only just been founded two years earlier and it was really early days in the broader public's awareness around bullying. We managed to get into a couple of schools and from there it was clear that the workshops were having an impact. The students were our greatest advocates.

We quickly discovered that we weren't building a business, we were building a movement. This movement has grown over the past 10 years and now we've reached hundreds of thousands of young Australians. It has exploded and expanded beyond anything that we ever imagined as two wide-eyed young girls.

PROJECT ROCKIT is constantly evolving

LUCY

When we launched PROJECT ROCKIT we developed the content ourselves and we felt really confident that our messaging was relevant and impactful for young people. Then social media exploded and we needed to evolve to keep PROJECT ROCKIT on point and credible. Social media has really changed the way people perceive the issue of bullying – it's now a 24/7 phenomenon that can really hit a person from all angles. Over the years, we have found ways to explore new issues within our existing model and methodology, but we have also had to adapt with the ever-changing digital space. The process continues to evolve, but we've worked really hard to set it up so that its core can be stable.

ROSIE

A pivotal milestone was when we launched our online curriculum in 2012. P-ROCK Online was our first online curriculum and a first for Australia. At this point in our journey, we were getting phone calls from people all over the country who wanted to be a part of the movement, and we knew it wasn't sustainable to send ourselves out there. We teamed up with digital partners who provided us with the online platform.

We launched the program and piloted it with more than 2,000 students. There were plenty of strengths to it and the pilot itself demonstrated that our program created positive attitudinal change, which was fantastic. We had lots of feedback, but there were also flaws. Now we're building version two, and we've learned so much from the first version.

We were lucky to secure a Social Innovations Grant from the Telstra Foundation that has allowed us to build version two, as well as a mobile app. We campaigned for two years to corporations so that we could get money to make the online program free for school students, so having Telstra as a partner has expanded our reach so much.

We have learned to rely on ourselves

LUCY

We have learned not to expect anything from anyone anymore. That sounds like an extremely negative belief, but actually it was empowering. We realised that while there are so many people and organisations who do want to support PROJECT ROCKIT, the best way to drive this movement forward is from within. For us there have been no shortcuts to growth, every step forward has been made through grind. By the time we secured funding from the Telstra Foundation, external support was no longer something we expected or relied on, which is why the grant was such a wonderful surprise!

Before Telstra, we have had a number of experiences of throwing everything behind opportunities that didn't come to fruition. At the end of the day it all came back to us though. Elbow grease, hard work, and relying on our core work got us through. Now we are able to work with huge companies, such as Facebook, Instagram and Twitter rather than just relying on them for support.

ROSIE

The phrase 'social enterprise' was a term we weren't familiar with when we started PROJECT ROCKIT, however that's exactly what we have been from the get-go. We decided to make it a commercial business, because if we had gone down the not-for-profit route we probably wouldn't be around one year later. By having a profit-for-purpose business model, it meant that we never had to rely on sponsorships or grant money and meant that we could get started and off the ground quickly.

There was a time when we thought that a particularly large corporate was going to take us on. When it didn't happen it felt unbearable. You put blood, sweat and tears into the business and then you face rejection. During these tough times, we are so lucky to have each other for support. Being an entrepreneur can be really lonely, but we have always had each other to rely on. Being sisters has given me an incredible wealth of drive. I have been answerable not just to myself, but to someone else as well.

Our staff are empowered by our mission

ROSIE

The key to PROJECT ROCKIT's success is our tight-knit, incredible team of passionate and talented young people. Building the PROJECT ROCKIT family was the first challenge of scaling. We set about finding other young people who could deliver the face-to-face workshops in schools. Finding the right people who are passionate about social justice, are great public speakers, and who are cool and credible was really challenging. Standing in front of 200 high school students is a tough gig! Now we have built an amazing team.

What I've learned is that it's not about 'teaching' your vision, it's about bringing people on board with your vision. At PROJECT ROCKIT, we all have equal input. We're all just as invested in the vision and in creating a better world for young people. Frankly, you wouldn't even make it through the P-ROCK front door if you didn't share that belief and the drive to make it happen.

LUCY

Our team is our most valued asset, so it's really important that we channel all of our support into making sure they're well looked after. When you're so passionate about the work that you're doing, it's so easy for these kinds of areas to slip.

The thing I love most about the opportunity that we have to offer our team at PROJECT ROCKIT is the mission to empower young people to stand up and really change the issue of bullying in school, online and beyond. Our teams are great examples of that. Before we thought our mission was only about empowering school students. Now PROJECT ROCKIT has been around long enough that those school students have finished school and now they're looking at the ways they can have impact on the wider world.

We've learned to practice what we preach

LUCY

The biggest thing that PROJECT ROCKIT has forced me to develop is an awareness of the balance between being humble and promoting the cause that I believe in. Like many young women, I've been raised to be humble at all times and never threatening to others. One of the challenges that I've found being a young woman in business is being assertive enough to push our cause above others. There have definitely been times in the past where we have been treated differently in the business world because of our gender, age and attitudes.

I started to realise that in order for me to truly live this mission and pursue it, I needed to advocate for it in my own life. I had to push myself to be a better role model. I had to 'woman up' and change my attitude, so I could be a better leader in the organisation.

ROSIE

A lot of people out there, particularly women, feel this 'imposter syndrome'. We're paranoid that someone's going to figure out that we don't deserve to be here or that we don't really know what we're doing. The realisation that this a common experience and that many people don't know exactly what they're doing all the time is incredibly comforting. We have met so many other people trying to develop a successful business, but with a social purpose. The momentum behind PROJECT ROCKIT and this movement we've created is so big now, that at times it feels like we're the elders in this social enterprise space.

There are so many young people who are starting businesses effecting social change, whether it's around gender and sexuality, poverty, climate change, refugee rights, animal welfare or any other of the issues we humans are struggling with. They're now coming to us and asking for support. This has really helped me feel like we deserve to be in this space and it's really rewarding to offer any support and guidance that we can.

Rosie's and Lucy's advice for startups

LUCY

If the idea for PROJECT ROCKIT had happened now rather than 10 years ago, we might never have gotten started. We would surely have been so fearful of all the problems and challenges that have stood in our way and so daunted by how much we had to learn. Not knowing was a blessing really.

Do you want to know the biggest advantage of starting PROJECT ROCKIT when we were so young? We just did it.

The biggest piece of advice I would give to anyone with a big idea is to get started. The rest can be learned along the way. It will be hard and you might make mistakes, embarrass yourself or straight out fail, but it also might just work.

ROSIE

I second that. Planning is important, but it can be paralysing. Taking even the smallest step towards action is helping to create your momentum. You don't have to have all the answers before you begin. If you don't know something, find someone who knows about it. There is always somebody out there who is willing to help you. You're never alone. You can always walk back down the path or change directions, but if you don't get started you're just going nowhere.

Rosie and Lucy's market

Rosie and Lucy remind us that as entrepreneurs build and scale businesses, these businesses in turn build the entrepreneurs. The feedback loop makes the entrepreneurial journey incredibly dynamic. If we think of these changes we see the *world changing* – and this external change includes:

1. The external environment (including the social, cultural, political, economic, legal and natural situations surrounding a firm and its industry).

2. The industry structures and dynamics (such as its suppliers, buyers, competitors, substitutes and complements).

3. The customer (the segments, the expectations, as well as the customers themselves).

Also, we know that the business changes (it grows, but also changes strategy, its resources and capabilities, its vision, the management, the reporting, and so on). At the same time we see the entrepreneur change (they grow older, wiser, more experienced, more successful, they have hardships, lose confidence, gain in confidence...). Everything changes.

Remember that your business will impact you – sometimes positively, as Rosie and Lucy notice, sometimes negatively – so remain mindful of these changes and how they impact your life and those around you.

What are the key takeouts from Rosie and Lucy Thomas?

I STARTED TO REALISE THAT IN ORDER FOR ME TO TRULY LIVE THIS MISSION AND PURSUE IT, I NEEDED TO ADVOCATE FOR IT IN MY OWN LIFE. I HAD TO PUSH MYSELF TO BE A BETTER ROLE MODEL.

I HAD TO 'WOMAN UP' AND CHANGE MY ATTITUDE SO I COULD BE A BETTER LEADER IN THE ORGANISATION.

LAUREN SILVERS

FOUNDER AND CEO OF GLAMAZON

Glamazon allows users to choose from a range of available appointments at luxury salons and book and pay for them instantly on its app. It was inspired by the convenience of Uber and is the brainchild of Lauren Silvers, who didn't let being a non-tech founder stop her from developing a new marketplace that could revolutionise the beauty industry.

My grandfather came to Australia with nothing. He's a Holocaust survivor and escaped the war. He describes 'luck' as an ability to spot an opportunity. You have to have your ear tuned into what's going on around you to be able to take advantage of those opportunities.

We have smart business people in my family. We always talk about new business ideas and inventions. When I came up with the idea for Glamazon, I had to pitch the idea to my Dad and my grandfather to show them that I knew what I was doing. I wasn't going to be earning a salary for god knows how long, so I was actually reaching out and asking for their support.

I've been building on my financial literary skills since I started my first business – a dog-walking business called Puppy People – when I was nine years old. I created fliers and dropped them in my neighbours' letterboxes, and walked a group of dogs every afternoon after school. Then, when I was 12 or 13 years old, I made pillows and sold them at the Bondi Markets.

Before I started Glamazon, I worked in PR and had a great relationship with my boss, so I was doing things that were probably outside the role of being just an account manager, I was developing business skills along the way.

It all started when I was in a meeting

I came up with the concept of Glamazon when I was in a meeting one day. I really wanted a blow-dry for the event that evening, but I had no way of leaving the meeting to call a salon. It occurred to me that there should be an easy way to book into any salon and pay for it.

We left the meeting and ordered an Uber and it just came to me all at once that I could create a similar app. I've had friends who worked at Uber so I was able to get some insights into the tech startup scene and just talking about it lit a fire inside me.

So I went to Start-Ups 101, held by the City of Sydney, and learnt how to get this business off the ground. I knew the idea would require technology, so I looked for people who could build the app. I have always believed in outsourcing my weaknesses and focusing on my strengths.

I moved back home and used my savings to get started. I quickly got a mentor – Robert Kawalsky, the co-founder and CEO of the interactive meeting and presentation platform Zeetings. He had built an app before and has been in the startup scene for a long time. I found people really wanted to help me and I started getting a supportive crew around me. They helped me find developers. I also quickly created an advisory board that consisted of people with skills that I needed to grow the business. I call them my 'dream factory'. We get together once a month and make dreams happen.

Initially, I had made a couple of mistakes. Like I went to an app agency and got them to scope out the app and I paid them $3,000 up front. It wasn't until I made that mistake that I really started asking people around me, 'how do you find a developer?' Luckily, Robert had just built an app called Tonight! and he knew exactly who to go to.

One thing I had learnt was not to worry about how the app looked or how pretty it was. I needed to create a functioning product that people would go to because it worked well. Development is key to the success of this business. That's what really prompted me to look for the best developers I could find and I was okay with paying a premium for that service.

Robert's introduction meant they gave me mates' rates and I kept promising them more work, and would direct other people to them. Business is about give and take. You can take something, but you've got to always be giving back.

Facebook helped me validate my idea

I came up with the idea for Glamazon early in 2013, and in October I quit my job to focus on the business full-time. In the beginning, I didn't know whether girls would really relate to my idea. I wasn't sure if they were experiencing the same frustration as me, so I decided to build a beta and do some testing while I was still in my job.

I put together a closed group of girls on Facebook and asked them to invite a colleague or family friend, so it was unbiased. I had 200 girls – 100 that I knew and 100 that I didn't know.

My developers built a really basic website. On the back end was a Google document that was connected to the website and a data entry form. I called 10 salons every morning to find out their availability for the day, then I put the information into this form, which spat out a URL. I copied and pasted that URL into this Facebook group, and when the girls clicked on it, it would show the availability at all these salons. They could click 'book now' for any appointment they wanted, and then put in their first name, last name and mobile number, and press 'book'. That email would go straight to me and I would manually book them in at the salon and the girls would then receive a confirmation email.

It looked like it was all automatic, but it was me manning a desk and waiting for emails to come through, and rushing around asking the salons to fit them in if they could. In those two weeks or so we booked 49 appointments and generated more than $1,500 for the salons. I thought, 'if I can do this in two weeks, I can create enough demand to make people want to book something'. Even if it was an impulse purchase, I knew the response had been positive. That was a real 'lightbulb moment' for me.

Every day I would also source relevant up-to-date beauty content for the girls to read. I strived to become an authoritative voice in beauty – that was really important to me. By providing them with connections to beauty services and also inspirational content and beauty trends, it became about them then 'booking the look', using the link I provided. It's about a complete circle – a whole journey of discovery.

The next challenge was figuring out how to curate thousands of different types of appointments offered by multiple salons into a simplified process. The user experience was a huge priority to me and a lot of research went into working out how my customers prefer to search. That involved considering what time clients wanted, what service they wanted, then it was about obtaining credit card details. It was a big feat to get that process right.

We did so many different progress maps, but we finally got the one we wanted and went into development. While that was happening – which took about four months – I on-boarded lots of salons and got the word out.

Good connections really helped

I had a really good connection at Joh Bailey salon, because my mum went to school with one of the founding partners. I had a meeting with her and she said they would give it a go and support me. Once I had that, I leveraged the relationship to sign on more salons. My strategy was, if I could get 10 of the most elite salons in Sydney, it would all fall into place and, actually, it worked.

Then my outbound sales became redundant and it was all about managing inbound sales, because people involved in the beauty industry all talk to each other. During that four month period I thought, 'I want to only on-board 40 salons in total, because I want to be able to manage supply and demand. If I take on too many they're not going to get any bookings and if I don't get enough salons I might have too many customers'. Financial modelling really helps with that sort of thing. You go, 'okay, for every 126 downloads you can on-board a new salon'. We came up with these metrics.

After I signed on the salons I contacted a few publications, particularly local papers. I'm a local Bondi girl and and all my salons were in the Eastern Suburbs to start off with, so I knew they would be interested in the story. A lot of the time I thought of the angle and managed to secured quite a bit of coverage. That really helped to solidify our brand in that area.

We researched different tech solutions

Initially, we thought, 'okay, salons need new business so let's provide them with a booking system that can do that'. But it was difficult to convert them to a new system and effectively change salon behaviours. We quickly realised this idea was not hugely scalable. We started researching different tech solutions that integrated with different technologies instead.

That's when the game kind of started to change – when appointments were definitely accurate and when salons didn't have to change their behaviour to be on the app.

Eventually, we came up with some ideas and just went for it. By that stage we were already taking 20 per cent commission off every transaction, so we were generating revenue and had a bit in the kitty. We also explored sweat-equity deals with the people who were already involved, saying, 'look, we really want to make this work, do you believe in it as much as we do?' and trying to get people in whichever way we could without having to pay them.

It was a lot of hassle and there were a lot of really low points where I thought I might give up. It's natural to think that way, but I pushed through and every new booking I get truly inspires me to keep going. I want to get as many girls using the platform as possible, so I can expand and think about how I can connect them with more lifestyle service providers such as fitness, health and wellness.

Since we launched in June, 2014, we've grown to include salons in Newcastle, and a small number of salons in Melbourne and Brisbane. When we sign on salons outside where we're targeting our marketing, it's really up to the salon to tell their customers how the app works. They become like your little sales rep, which is exciting.

We're increasing efficiency because they don't have to answer as many phone calls or wait to process payments at the end of an appointment. We automatically transfer funds every 48 hours, so they're reimbursed pretty quickly.

Social media is fantastic for us

My target audience is 18 to 30 year old women. We find that 18 to 24-year-olds use the app religiously. The ones in my age bracket, 25 to 30, who we're also targeting, have already got someone they've gone to for quite a while or they're not as in tune with changing things as much as the younger kids. But having celebrities validate Glamazon through social media helps us convince girls that, 'oh, this is actually an easier way to connect with salons. It's just like Uber'.

Facebook and Instagram have been really good avenues for us. We can be a visual brand, because people want to show how their hair looks after it has been done or how their nails look. Other girls find it inspirational.

Traditional PR has also been good for us, from a brand elevation perspective, but we can't really track the downloads or users that come from that. We like using marketing and advertising avenues where we can track and measure the results. It's important to know our acquisition costs.

Getting your marketing formula down pat takes a while – it takes exploring a multitude of different techniques. We've done street posters, flyers, a whole range of stuff, but it really comes down to tracking the success of those. We tried 12 different strategies, tested each one for at least two weeks and looked at the data. We found what our key strategies were and what worked the best. No surprise, it's digital.

I believe in strength before speed

I'd love to have a whole team of account managers, but I believe in strength before speed, which means strengthening our business model and making it so tight and so valuable that we can accelerate quicker when the time is right.

One of our values is to operate with kindness and respect. This is going to sound cheesy, but being kind to one another is really important to me. Sometimes you can get an upset customer, but the challenge is turning that into something positive so they walk away thinking, 'oh my god, I love Glamazon'.

It's a challenge to get things done all the time though, because as the founder and CEO I have to focus on business development and business strategy. The business definitely relies on my input, but I think we're on the right track and our monthly board meetings make sure we're realising our dreams.

The business is like a child of mine. When it's not doing well it's almost like a sick child. I feel like it flows through my veins; it's like part of me. People talk about work-life balance all the time, but there's no such thing for me, it's all the same thing.

Lauren's market

Lauren demonstrates how to build a business around the concept of 'ask, try, do, reflect'. She is not shy of asking questions of herself and others (whether they're her mentor, suppliers, clients, customers, or members of her 'dream factory'). With this insight and expertise, Lauren tests her understandings. For example, she tested her technology and business flow through Facebook; she piloted the way Glamazon integrates with salons, and she even trialled the business model region by region.

After learning from those trials, she delivers at scale. Throughout this cycle of development, Lauren reflects and is mindful, always communicating and discussing with others. She takes care to reciprocate the help and care she receives, and so builds relationships. The industry insight she develops through this cycle of learning is invaluable. Ask, Try, Do, Reflect!

ask
try
do
REFLECT

NOTES

SHANSHAN WANG

FOUNDER AND CEO OF ROAM TECHNOLOGIES

A chance sighting of a child in a park, encumbered by a heavy oxygen tank, affected product designer ShanShan Wang so deeply that she knew she had to build something better. What she hadn't planned on, was that her revolutionary oxygen device would have applications far beyond the medical industry.

I was in my fourth year at the University of New South Wales when I was walking to my car one day. I still remember the child and her mother. Usually, you expect a child to be happily running around the park, swinging on the swings, being energetic and having fun. This child had an oversized object on the ground and wasn't on the swings. You could almost feel how draining it was for them to be outside. When I walked closer, the object turned out to be an enormous oxygen cylinder and the small child was attached to it.

I remember thinking, 'why is an oxygen cylinder attached to the child?' It made no sense. I turned up to St Vincent's Hospital's respiratory department, out of the blue, and asked a lot of questions about why someone hadn't built something better. I knew I probably could.

From then, I read more articles, interviewed and dedicated my final year thesis on *Roam – a lightweight Oxygen Cylinder*.

I didn't realise how big an impact the device was having (even at a conceptual phase) until people started contacting me and asking when I was going to have it ready for market. The plan is to have a pre-production unit and currently, that's nearly ready. If we decide to put it on market at that point, there would be marketing to do and distribution, logistics and a bunch of other challenges to solve.

One hundred years to make a difference

I've got 100 years to live an 'optimal' life, hopefully. Within that hundred years, I want to do something that has a positive impact on the world. Some tutors back at university

said, 'don't build this, because you don't have enough experience in this area', which is fair enough. I saw it from their point of view. They hoped I'd go into the industry, get some experience, figure out how to do it, then think about doing something as crazy as this.

But I thought I should try to do it and prove them wrong. The only way I could figure out how was to take one step at a time – break it down into smaller chunks that I could understand. First step was, how do I build it? I needed an engineer, so I emailed people on LinkedIn and hoped they would be able to help. A couple of people got back to me.

Then I asked them if they would build it and how much it would cost. Some prices were crazy, obviously. Some were relatively okay and some wanted more information. The people who wanted more information, I asked them if they could refer me to a better person who would love to do something like this.

I wrote more than 100 emails. I asked a lot of wrong questions at the beginning. The first couple of guys must have thought I was completely insane. Then I figured I should simplify it and objectively tell them what I needed. And then I sent them *that* email.

If I was referred to someone who was 10 or 15 times smarter than me and talked about something that I didn't know about – like physics or chemistry – then I was like 'great, you're hired'. If you know that area, then most likely that person's probably not a good fit. But if they see things beyond what you're seeing, then hopefully, they can help you navigate where you need to go. That's my theory.

Building a business

I'm slowly getting the idea of how to create and build a business. I associate an entrepreneur with someone who's successful, who has done it. At my company Roam Technologies, we have so far built a proof of concept, which proves our theories, but I haven't commercialised anything yet, so I don't really consider myself an entrepreneur.

There's a lot of red tape involved in getting a product from the concept idea through to production and then on to the market. At the moment, we're evaluating ISO compliances. We're sorting out all the paperwork, getting all our ducks in a row. We know there are people out there with a lot of money who would love to invest, but it's not just the money side of it – we want them to be involved and believe in what we're doing. They also need to be a bit crazy, because what we're doing is not just innovative – we want to change the industry.

I know how to design a product that's going to sell like crazy, but when we started, I didn't know the business strategy side of it. I wish I'd done more business classes and talked to different sorts of people back at uni. I also didn't know about commerce, finance and the marketing, which is where my co-founder Natalie Ho comes in. I have known Natalie for over 13 years and we went to high school together.

Matt Shepit is our senior mechanical engineer and Julia Walker is our chemical and materials engineer. They handle the technical side of the product. Even Matt says there were some areas that he didn't understand, so he found Julia through his network. Ben Browning is the business development director – he understands the business, marketing and technical aspects – and Marco Tallarida is an industrial designer, who understands plastic mass-manufacturing.

Natalie introduced me to our current mentor Paul Riley, who has been involved with building businesses from ground up, private equity and capital raising. He is currently the CEO of Sphere Healthcare and advises me about what I'm building. I have two other mentors as well: Dr Philip Boughton, a biomedical engineering, lecturer and program manager at Sydney University; and Jo Burston, the founder and CEO of Inspiring Rare Birds. Their advice, guidance and support are invaluable to what we're building. I can't thank them enough.

If you can collaborate and believe in what you're building – even if you don't know how to get there – something amazing will eventually happen. I want to hire a bunch of smart people, put them together in a room and watch the magic happen. I look for people who are hungry and want to build something big. If you provide them with that opportunity, and platforms of where you need to get to, then you're bound to create something amazing.

Everybody involved in the business is excited by what they're doing. Wanting to change the world for the better is also a hunger. I don't care what everybody thinks, there are always going to be haters out there. I'm going to do it because I believe in this idea. People see that and they think, 'wow, if she could do that, why can't I?' It's one of those things where you just go for it and see what happens.

When I hit a wall, all I can do is laugh about it, take a step back, think about it, figure out what I did wrong, then pick another direction. One of my mentors said to me, 'life is like a y-shaped road – you can go in this direction, make a wrong step and it's okay. Just take a step back and go down the other road'.

In the classroom

I had a really good design and technology teacher back in high school. I'd come up with these crazy things and he'd say, 'that's a pretty cool idea, we should do that'. When I went into industrial design in university, I found a design mentor, who was a free thinker and he taught me more about form and function – how to make something look good, how to make something start. If he designed a curve in a certain way, he knew it was going to have an impact on the person buying the product.

There are so many impact areas that could be improved, and it's not impossible to do. I've realised nothing's actually impossible. It's hard, but it's not impossible. You may be crazy, but you know you'll get there. Anything is possible when you get a bunch of crazy people together and you just do it.

I don't work by numbers. It's more about having the right feeling and a good team backing you. When I was doing my graduation project, and it was on display and everyone was looking at it, this woman walked up to me and shook my hand. She said, 'this is amazing, I'd love to use something like this, please build something like this'. That, for me meant more than the marks I received, because that was someone I could help, and that's really what I wanted to do.

I want to be remembered for something that I did – something that had an impact on the world. At the end of the day, all that I really want to do is just build this. For me, it's about personal fulfilment. By the time I turn 30, 40 or 50, I'm not going to be doing the same thing I was doing in my twenties. I just turned 24 years old, so I'll at least give it a go and see what happens.

We apply design science technology to build new and better technology that will advance humanity together. Isn't that changing the world? I haven't figured out my purpose yet. All I know is, I want to do something that has a lasting impact.

Shan's tips for uni students

• If you're at university, talk to a business person or someone outside your degree, because they will know something you don't and could help you out in the long-run. I spoke to people who understood business.

• Don't limit yourself by thinking that by the end of your time at university you're just going to get a job. There are more things to the world than just that.

• Learn as much as you can and network like crazy. The university resources are infinite. I still go back to the university and borrow books. Having a student card is the best thing. When you exit university, you don't get access to it, which is one of the reasons why I returned to tutor in design. I get a staff card now and I get access. The people there also love what you do and the tutors are there to help and guide you. Eventually, you're going to have to go back there and ask them a couple of things.

Local works best

Sometimes it's better to have things made locally than to try and have components produced overseas. I have a ton of examples of this in my business, like when we were engineering some components from China. It's tough to communicate with them if you don't know Chinese and you're talking about screw threads, and trying to figure out if what they're describing is going to work. They've got their own standards and you've got yours.

It was relatively inexpensive to go down that route and although it's worthwhile trying, I realised we were better off having it made locally by someone we knew, who could have it done within the day, instead of waiting two or three weeks for a part. You've also got to get that part shipped and through customs, and you don't even know if it's going to be right or not. Whereas the guys here in Australia know exactly what you're on about, because they speak the same language and they have the same skills.

What is Shan's strategy?

Shan gives excellent insight into how she, over time, is crafting her business strategy. Notice how this strategy seeks to align her vision and competence with the external situation (particularly the needs of potential users of her product). Elements of the strategy include articulating:

1. With whom she should collaborate (the engineers, manufacturers, technical experts, gatekeepers, distributors, and so on).

2. What differentiates her offerings (the unique and protectable compact, light and secure design, as well as the product's premium quality and specifications).

3. The product categories and segments she will serve and where (people anywhere in the world who require portable, but lightweight and secure gas).

4. When she will develop her offerings (narrow specialist offerings first, such as for children, then more broadly for anyone needing portable gas).

5. How she will obtain her returns (premium pricing, premium offering). Her challenge is then make sure these individual elements of strategy are aligned and integrated into a powerful whole, ensuring she can sustainably and profitably build her business.

I'VE REALISED NOTHING'S ACTUALLY IMPOSSIBLE. IT'S HARD, BUT IT'S NOT IMPOSSIBLE. YOU MAY BE CRAZY, YOU MAY BE INSANE, BUT YOU KNOW YOU'LL GET THERE BY THE END OF IT.

NOTES

phronesis.academy

What I learnt from ShanShan Wang that could affect my business

DEBORAH SYMOND

FOUNDER AND DIRECTOR OF MODE SPORTIF

Photographer: Holly Blake

Deborah Symond saw an opportunity to fill a niche in the Australian women's fashion market. After two years of hard work and planning Mode Sportif was launched. This luxury leisure and activewear fashion destination goes beyond an online store, promoting a holistic lifestyle in an aspirational sense. Mode Sportif continues to exceed Deborah's expectations as women in Australia and overseas buy into the lifestyle and Mode Sportif story.

We launched Mode Sportif in October, 2014. It was a project that was two years in the making. My career was based in the fashion industry and before launching Mode Sportif I was working specifically in e-commerce and buying. It was important that I took the time to fully research the market. This spanned over six months and involved travelling through Europe and the United States, where I had met with a lot of people, particularly in the active workspace. That was where my interest was first sparked – this coupled with the knowledge that it is the largest growing sector in the apparel market. From here, I spent another six months researching which brands would make the right mix for the Mode Sportif concept, meeting designers and really solidifying the concept.

At Mode Sportif we wanted to take our concept a step further than just an activewear destination. We are curating the best of leisurewear and activewear brands from around the world, from leading international designers. We want to own the 'off-duty' space. This is where I introduced leisurewear/weekend-wear into the overall concept of Mode Sportif.

We want our customers to buy into the leisure or active category, or both, and encourage for the two to mix – taking you confidently from the studio to the street and vice versa. It's really important for us to be able to give our customers guidance on how to build their casual wear wardrobe and how to incorporate this dress code into their life, through our interactive content on the website.

I want Mode Sportif to be so much more than a store. It's about creating the community and building a lifestyle, not just selling a product. We write content around health and wellbeing, new workout styles, beauty tips, and style advice.

Mode Sportif is a holistic community and a place where people can go to access that lifestyle. I personally live and breathe it, and absolutely love it. That's where the idea for Mode Sportif came from. There was a gap in the market at that time and I wanted to chase that before it was too late. There has been a lot of interest, because it's a different concept. We've got amazing brands and it's something that's exciting the Australian marketplace, and the international marketplace. The next 12 months is about nailing what we've got going on in Australia. We want to tighten our brand mix and grow the brand across the country before we invest in the international market.

Mode Sportif is built on a strong brand story

I spend a lot of time choosing the right brands – we now have 50 on board. We've also spent a lot of hours getting the branding right, so we could express our concept clearly and consistently to the people we wanted to partner with, and so they could share the vision that we have for the site. We have some of the best brands in the world and I've worked on getting those relationships to the point where we now have ongoing brand partners.

That strong brand experience flows from the website and products we sell, through to the delivery and distribution experience for the customer. It's really important to manage the complete end-to-end experience for them. I made the decision before we launched to not go with a third party warehouse to distribute the stock at this early stage. We warehouse all of our own stock and we dispatch from there. We sell premium products and it was extremely important for me to have complete control at this stage over the complete customer experience from beginning to end.

We have a team who package and write personal notes to each of our customers. It's a highly personal, reliable experience and this is one of the reasons that we are seeing such growth in our sales in only our first year since launch. Online fashion has really boomed, but the level of customer service is not there. We are trying to change that up and give our customers great service, even though we don't have a bricks and mortar store.

Getting the technology right is an ongoing challenge

Technology has been the biggest challenge for us – building a custom website and ironing out all the technical difficulties of operating an online store. I had no idea the development of the site could be so difficult and labour intensive. There are so many things about the custom build that have allowed us to be different, which is what I wanted and why we went down that path. Websites and e-commerce is constantly changing and evolving, and it's really important for us to be extremely flexible.

I had to put in a lot of research to make sure we were making the right decision to build our website and that it was on the right platform. We need to be updating the website daily, looking at analytics to decide which direction we will move in, based on the back end of the site. We look at customer behaviour and respond to this information, whether it means new development, changes, updates or new design.

Going with an open source solution could have been easier for everyone involved, but in saying that there are a lot of things we wouldn't have been able to do. It would have been the easy option, but I don't know it would have been the better option. I'm happy with how we've done it, but it has presented its own challenges.

We have an online and offline strategy

We've got a strategy that is both online and offline at the moment. Online takes time to grow in terms of SEO and traffic, so we've supported that with offline events. We're working across Australia to introduce new people to our brand. We don't have the presence of a historical brand. It's really important for us to build a strong presence in Australia, and our long-term plan is to grow the business internationally.

Recently, we held a number of health and wellbeing experiences across Australia, in beautiful locations and private homes. We invited our customers and opinion leaders to a private pilates session, followed by a healthy banquet lunch, then a styling and shopping session. It has been hugely successful for the business in terms of sales, branding and positioning.

Mode Sportif also prides itself on giving our customers a VIP experience in our studio, where customers can book appointments to visit us for a personal styling session. This allows the customer to try items on with one of the team. That level of one-on-one care sets us apart as an online store.

We have a strategy that spans across Facebook and Instagram, and we also work with Pinterest. Facebook is an incredible tool for driving sales for our business. Every week we post new blogs about health, fashion and styling that promotes the lifestyle of the brand, and our customers really respond to this content.

I have a team of passionate brand advocates

My team of eight staff are passionate about the brand. You've got to be really passionate about it, because this is not the kind of job where you can come in at nine and leave at five. We are a website that operates 24 hours a day. It's really important for me that the team is passionate and believe in the concept. It can be a crazy fast paced environment and every day is different. The team are leaders in the Australian fashion industry and they wholeheartedly believe in the Mode Sportif concept – they live and breathe it.

I look for leaders in the industry who are going to bring their skill sets to areas of our business. Working in a startup means we've got the ability to make changes easily and that's something I find really exciting. An idea can be thought of in the morning and by lunchtime we can be well into bringing it to life. Working with people who are so clever and savvy in their field, and who thrive on the fast paced nature of the business, is really important to me.

Being a business owner has taught me so much

I wasn't aware of this before I started Mode Sportif, but as a startup owner you do so many tasks and things that you never thought you would or could ever do. You test your limits and learn to know your limits as well. There are things about yourself that you never would have known you were capable of and it gives you a confidence and strength that you can apply to your personal life as well. Living and working with purpose is just as relevant to my personal life as it is to my business life.

I am all about celebrating the wins. I am very much a glass half-full kind of person and not the type to dwell on something that hasn't gone well. I look at the mistakes and learn from them. When things go really well, that's when you need to pat yourself on the back and acknowledge the hard work that you're doing. On the flip side, when things are at their worst that's when you really need to rise to the occasion. You need to be there for your team, you need to be there for yourself, and you need to be pushing as hard as you can for the business. There is no time to dwell on negative things. You need to be strongest at those moments and that's something I think about every day.

Mentors have been a great source of inspiration and guidance for me. You can learn something from every person you meet. I talk to a lot of people who have experience in specific areas when I am mulling over a major decision. My dad has been an amazing mentor for me throughout this entire process. He understands a lot about the industry as well. He has been through everything before. Anything that I bring to the table, he's been there, done that and has advice. He's not only a constant guide, but also an inspiration.

There are two major things you need before you make a commitment to a new business: passion for the project and a solid business plan. I'm so passionate about this project. I really believe in it and I know that it's going to be amazing. I don't think I could do it without believing in it so much. You also need a clear structure around how it's going to work and why. I've talked to a lot of young women who have amazing goals and passions, and I say, go for it. Do the groundwork, but go for it. Don't be scared of what's going to go wrong. Things will go wrong and it might not work, but have the confidence to give it your best shot, which is what I'm doing, too.

What is Deborah's strategy?

Deborah has described how a successful strategy must align multiple situations, aspirations, and capabilities. Identifying the elements of strategy (essentially the 'who?', 'what?', 'where?', 'when?' and 'how?' questions. Also see page 122, 'What is Shan's strategy?') is only part of the analysis entrepreneurs must undertake before they articulate a powerful strategy.

As well as ensuring the elements of the strategy are integrated, the entrepreneur checks this integrated strategy aligns the different aspects of business. The strategy must align the enterprise's resources and capabilities, with the entrepreneur's vision and purpose, and with the external environment (the customers' needs and expectations, industry structures and the dynamics of the environment. Notice the effort taken by the team at Mode Sportif to do this. It is an ongoing exercise, not something that is planned and documented once.

NOTES

16

LE HO

OWNER AND DIRECTOR OF CAPITAL CITY WASTE SERVICES

Le Ho shows how she took her waste management company from a $700,000 turnover in 2010, to just under $10 million in 2015.

My parents fled Vietnam in a rickety fishing boat in the late 1970s, at the end of the Vietnam War. At the time, I was only 18 days old. Nobody knew if we'd survive to reach another land or if we would die at sea. My family were one of the lucky few who survived and eventually settled in Australia. I feel fortunate for this opportunity that I've been given. I feel that if I don't achieve anything in my life, then I would have wasted this opportunity that Australia has given me and that my parents have risked our lives for nothing.

Growing up, my parents always told me that, as a female, I should study hard, get a degree and get married to a good husband who would look after me. This was the dream of a new life in a new country.

I knew though, that if I had big enough dreams and worked hard enough, I could achieve them. Australia was a land of equal opportunities, and anything was possible, as long as you believed in your dreams. If I set my goals to achieve 100 per cent, and I only reached 80 per cent, it would be 80 per cent better than if I had not set myself any goals at all. At 21 years old, I decided to leave university and begin my business career.

When I was 28, I started working in the waste management industry. The first few years in this business were extremely difficult for me. The waste management industry is male dominated and I was a female owner with little experience. I would often turn up to social events and be the only female at the table. I used to feel extremely intimidated, but now I find it quite empowering. I'm in my thirties, running a waste management company that's financially successful, respected and recognised within New South Wales. Many people who have been working within the waste management industry for 40 to 50 years have been surprised by the growth of my business.

I showed I could turn the business around

When I took over the business in 2010, it was losing quite a lot of money. I had to let staff go, take on their roles myself and change over the existing drivers. Getting through the first year of business is a highlight in my life, because I had demonstrated I could turn the business around, could change the thinking of my industry peers and make a footprint for myself in my business.

Until two years ago, Capital City didn't have a website. I didn't have sales reps on the road, so all my customers were from word-of-mouth referrals. I'm not that IT literate, so we've never been big at promoting the business through the internet and social media. If it's a customer who has been with me for a long time, they've got my mobile number and I'll always pick up the calls at the weekend. If I'm passing a customer's business premises I'll try to take five minutes to go in and say 'hi'. I'd say 90 per cent of customers who were with me at the beginning are still with Capital City today.

When the company was turning over $1.5 million I was still running the office from the boot of my car. I didn't have an office. In the morning, I'd wake up between 6am and 12pm and do a waste collection run. Then, from 12pm to 5pm, I'd change my clothes and go to meetings and find new customers. In the evenings, between 6pm and 1am, I did accounts and returned emails. I did that for two years. Our turnover now is just under $10 million.

Physically, I was exhausted, but I didn't have time to feel tired. I was motivated to make the business work, because there were a lot of people expecting me to be unsuccessful. It wasn't all about the monetary gain; it was the challenge of making it work.

I've got the best staff in the industry

I've been successful, because I've got some of the best people in the industry helping me drive the business. I know my staff share my same vision, so their hearts are in the company and they'll work above and beyond what's expected of them.

Everyone in my business has something good and unique to offer. It's a continual learning and growing process for me. If we're not united as a company and we're not united with each other, then we can't go out and battle the world.

I don't like to micro manage people. Everyone knows their role. I've never set a KPI or have sat down and given out a list of targets to hit. I often have open discussions about the issues we encounter and how we can get through them. We talk about where we can seek new business, maintain current customer satisfaction and new work we're gaining. It's exciting. I want to set people up to succeed, hence their mental drive for success is extremely important so one day, if they want to set up a business, they can.

One of the most difficult things about running a business is always ensuring staff are happy and that you're leading well. If I come in unhappy and drained of energy, it's going to affect my team. Instead, I come to work, I look at what we've achieved and where we're going, rather than what we haven't achieved and what we haven't yet accomplished. I still love what I do – I love the people I work with and the people that I work for. It's a joyous thing.

I have big plans for the business

In the next six months, we'll expand to Victoria and then the other states will follow. It will be difficult, but the company already has its backbone in New South Wales, so it's not going to be like starting from scratch. Capital City was grown organically until now, so I believe the next stage of growth will come from acquisitions.

I only started raising capital about 18 months ago. I'm cautious about taking on loans. As the business has grown and made money, I've reinvested it to buy equipment. Perhaps I could have achieved the goals a lot faster, with a lot more risk, but I've chosen to go a lot more slowly, build a more solid foundation, without the risks.

We recently invested in a really good application, which is quite groundbreaking for our industry and it has won us some large contracts. You always have to keep your eyes and ears out for what the customer needs are – what the customer expectations are – and deliver a service that is above and beyond the industry level.

I don't have the internet at home

In the past 18 months I've stepped back a bit, so I have my weekends and I try to switch off when I get home. There's no internet connection there, apart from my phone and I don't watch a lot of TV either.

As a woman, you have to decide how to achieve the right work-life balance. I try to finish work at about 5pm (my phone is still on and I'm contactable 24/7 for emergencies), then I dedicate the evenings and weekends for my family.

My business is my baby, too. I've nurtured it from being a 'non-business' to being a successful, thriving company. At the end of the day, it's not just a business, it's part of me – it's part of my life.

Le's advice for startups

• Always dare to dream and always dare to make those dreams become reality. That's not saying you go into business blind – draw up a business plan, find out who will be supporting your business.

• Emotional support is really important. If you're around negative people every day your energy levels will be really low. If you're around positive people, who can share you vision, then you'll have your low days, but you can pick up the phone and ring your network of supporters. Quite often they can't help you, but if you can speak to someone who understands, then you'll feel 100 per cent better.

• Be honest and to treat your staff and customers with integrity. For me, my business is not all about monetary returns. What I get out at the end of the day is the satisfaction of happy customers and the privilege of working with such a great team. For me, it's the challenge of continually growing my business. There are weekends when I walk past streets and I see the footprint of my bins out there and I'm really happy about what I've achieved.

• You can have a really good day one day and make lots of money and then the next day your expenses go out the door. It's really important to always keep your costs in hand and always be aware of what they will be in the next one, two, three months, so you don't have any unexpected expenses.

Management and leadership

With insights including how to bootstrap and turnaround operations, Le gives particularly poignant advice about leadership. Notice how she is focused on people and creating multiple helpful relationships. She has built the right team, she draws on the right minds, and she creates shared purpose.

Le ensures that everyone is aware of their role (without requiring narrow KPIs), and she listens to what her team and her customers say. Leadership is not just about managing the profitability of the business, it is also about taking responsibility and setting the example. Capital City is flourishing because of Le's leadership.

WHEN THE COMPANY WAS TURNING OVER $1.5 MILLION I WAS STILL RUNNING IT FROM MY CAR. I DIDN'T HAVE AN OFFICE.

NOTES

BUILD YOUR TEA

17

JUSTINE FLYNN

CO-FOUNDER AND DIRECTOR OF THANKYOU

Photographer: Sebastian Avila

Justine Flynn and two of her friends, Daniel and Jarryd, wanted to change the world. With no experience, no business plan and no funding, these three young Australians set out in 2008 to create the social enterprise called Thankyou. Today their products fund aid programs around the world, allowing everyday Australians to be empowered to make a difference.

I really started to have a passion for business is when I was in Year 11. I was nominated to be in an Australian business competition which involved a group of 10 students being put in a team. My group's simulated business won and went on to compete in the nationals. That was my first taste of business success.

Thankyou started in 2008 when Daniel, my business partner and also now my husband, came across some hard-hitting facts about the world water crisis. At the time there were 900 million people that didn't have access to basic human rights like clean water, while Australians alone spent $600 million on bottled water annually. That's when the idea for Thankyou was born. We thought, 'what if we could create consumer products that would fund a solution for people in need?'

We started with bottled water and in seven years have grown to 35 products across three ranges – water, body care and food. Each range funds a different need it is associated with. For example, the water range funds safe water access, the food range funds access to immediate food aid and long-term food solutions and the body care range funds hygiene and sanitation programs.

Our charity partners give us reports and updates so we know that what's happening on paper is actually happening on the ground. We also visit the projects we are funding to see where the money is going.

At the beginning we were looking at whether we might start it as a charity, but there were already so many great charities out there and we didn't want to compete with the work they were doing. We also needed to make money and we needed to compete with all the other products on the shelf. We had to set up as a for-profit business that gives all the profit away, so that's how we're categorised as a social enterprise. The company is 100 per cent owned by the charitable trust and all the profits go into the trust.

Starting from nothing

Daniel and Jarryd were in their first year of university and I had just begun studying when we started Thankyou. Once we decided to focus on bottled water we went from factory to factory asking questions. We found out we needed $200,000 to cover the first run of production and we didn't have that. A mentor told Daniel, 'if the idea is good enough, the money will come', so we continued to go from factory to factory, because we believed in our 'why' so we needed to find the right partner who would support us.

By the time we got to the last factory and told them everything we wanted to do, the guy sat back in his chair, and he said, 'so you're telling me you don't want to do this for yourself? You don't want to make your own money, you want to help others?' He said he would do our first production run and we could pay him back after we sold it. This meant that we didn't need that startup money.

We had everything on the production side ready to go, but obviously the factory wouldn't run anything for us until we got a sale. We managed to get a 15 minute meeting with one of Australia's largest private beverage distributors. We walked out of that meeting with our first order of 50,000 bottles. It was surreal.

It was all happening so quickly and we hadn't done all the important administrative things that we needed to do for the business, which was going to cost about $20,000. Daniel met with one of his business mentors and shared the idea for Thankyou. He told him we had a factory, a sale and we were all ready to go, but that we needed $20,000. His mentor gave the money to us within a couple of days as a gift. That started the epic journey.

The rollercoaster ride began

We've faced many challenges along the journey. For the first shipment, we arranged for a case to be sent to Daniel's parents' garage – we were so excited, but as the guys pulled out the bottles their faces just went blank. The label was scrunched up all the way around to the point where it was unreadable on about a third of the pallet.
We had to call the distributor to tell him what happened and he was very upset. He had already sent it out Australia-wide and had to do a recall. Recalls ruin big brands and we weren't even a big brand yet. Luckily for us he gave us a second chance. It was the rockiest year.

Meanwhile, the three of us had part-time jobs. Daniel and Jarryd were traffic controllers, while I was working as a nanny. I would look after two little girls all day and juggle Thankyou and study around that. We were slogging our guts out. We were a year into the business when it pretty much went under. It was really hard and made us ask, 'why are we doing this?'

It wasn't an easy ride, but we were driven by the impact we could create. We visited the projects we had funded and heard stories from community members about how the water solution had changed their lives, and it renewed us and reminded us again of our 'why'.

I look back on it now and I learned more in those first three years than I did from my university degree. You can use those hurdles and challenges to break you or you can use them to make you. We were determined to let them make us.

We took some big risks that paid off

We always had plans for Thankyou to be more than water. For holistic and long-term sustainable change to happen there are other issues that need to be addressed, like sanitation and food aid, so we developed a body care and food range that would fund hygiene and sanitation programs and food aid for people in need.

The thing is, we knew that to make a bigger impact, we needed to get our products on the shelves in Australia's largest supermarkets. We'd spent years trying to get our water range in with no luck. Every time we had a meeting with them, they'd say, 'where's your million dollar marketing campaign?' and 'how do you know people will buy it?' So we came up with our Coles and Woolworths Campaign.

We booked meetings with both retailers, and the campaign was about asking our community to come with us to the meeting (figuratively speaking). We filmed a one-take video and uploaded it to YouTube (you can search, 'Thankyou Coles and Woolworths Campaign' to take a look at it) that unveiled the two new ranges and asked Australians to back the Thankyou movement by writing on Coles' and Woolworths' Facebook pages that if the retailers stocked Thankyou products, they'd buy it. It went off! Within days, thousands of people wrote or uploaded videos. Celebrities backed it. We got over 15 million media impressions, and in record time (within five hours after meeting) they both said 'yes'.

Oh and we may have flown helicopters around their head offices one week after the campaign launch (just as a gentle reminder).

A campaign that should have cost us over $100,000.00 cost us a tiny fraction of that. Because we focused on innovation and building momentum, we were able to get people on board to help sponsor the campaign and businesses that partnered with us to provide in-kind support.

If it failed, that campaign could have ruined our reputation. By taking that risk, it has actually helped us grow. We've given more to impact in this past year than we have in the previous six years and being in the supermarkets has helped that greatly.

Impact drives our business

We measure ourselves predominately by impact. In 2015 alone we gave $1.57 million to projects. When you hear the statistics every single one of those numbers is a person, a life and a story. To think that everyone who buys Thankyou products is empowering them to live life to the full and start to lift themselves out of poverty is just amazing.

At the same time there is still so much need out there. We have to keep going and we need to keep making a bigger impact. Someone in our team asked us what we wanted to tell our grandchildren about Thankyou. Daniel said he'd tell Jed, our little son, that poverty used to exist, but now it doesn't. The ultimate goal is to play a part in eradicating global poverty. It may seem like a pipe dream, but we see that it's possible.

We like to connect our consumers with the real impact that they're making. It's important for us to maintain integrity in how we share the stories, and also to protect the dignity of the people whose stories we're telling. We want to empower the everyday Australian to make a difference. To promote transparency we created a web-based app called Track Your Impact. Every single product we have has a unique code on it that when entered online shows you GPS coordinates of the solution the product is assigned to fund. If you sign in with your email or Facebook, we send you a report and photo of the solution once it has been completed.

We've built a team of like-minded people

We're really big on our culture and our team is really tight-knit. We want to make sure the team is unified and the staff honour and encourage each other.

We look for people who are solutions-focused; people who don't get consumed by restraints or things not going as planned. We also look for people who dream big. We say in our team that impossibility is only someone's opinions, not a fact. Even though it seems like it's impossible we try to find a way to make it happen.

There is a quote by Martin Luther King, Jr that goes, "All labour that uplifts humanity has dignity and importance, and should be undertaken with painstaking excellence". It's framed on the wall of our office and we live by it. We believe that the people we help and the people who buy our products deserve the best. And we believe that our business deserves the best. That inspiration has made a difference in our team, because they know they deserve the best that we can do for them.

I also think it's wise to never get to a point where you think you've made it. We believe we can learn anything from anyone and always encourage our team to continue to learn. That humility of learning from anyone, no matter who they are, is what can help you continue to grow.

I hear from a lot of people who have big dreams. I'm really big on anyone being able to achieve their dreams, but a lot of people are afraid to start. They fear the unknown or that they will fail, that they don't have enough experience or enough money. We had no experience, no money, no qualifications, but we just jumped in. We realised that we could keep going and we jumped again and again. Just jump into it and don't let fear or excuses hold you back.

Management and leadership

Justine, Daniel and Jarryd show some of the essential elements of managing resources and cash flows. Clearly, dollar revenues and costs impact the profitability of a business, but the timing of those dollars can be equally critical to success. Thankyou was able to start because the trio shortened the operating cash cycle and negotiated favourable terms with suppliers and buyers.

In addition to these timing-related bootstraps (such as obtaining advance payments, negotiating delayed payments to suppliers, deliberately choosing customers who pay quickly, and keeping a close eye on overdue accounts), we also see owner-related bootstrapping (such as withholding founders' salaries, working part-time in other businesses, using personal credit cards for business expenses) and they probably also leveraged joint-utilisation bootstrapping (bartering, sharing business locations and equipment, and so on). Successful entrepreneurs manage their resources prudently.

YOU CAN USE THOSE HURDLES AND CHALLENGES TO BREAK YOU OR YOU CAN USE THEM TO MAKE YOU.

WE WERE DETERMINED TO LET THEM MAKE US.

18

MIA McCARTHY

FOUNDER AND CEO OF YUMMIA

Photographer: Ryan Pike

149

Mia McCarthy started making bircher muesli in her kitchen four years ago. Since then her business Yummia, has outgrown three manufacturing premises and now her products are sold in 250 Woolworths stores across New South Wales, Victoria and Queensland. In 2016, she plans to start exporting to Asia. She's 26 years old.

I started making bircher muesli at home in 2011, as a hobby when I was at university. I was about 21 or 22 years old at the time. My Mum helped organise breakfast events at my sister's school and they ate bircher muesli at the events, then we started eating it at home.

I did some research and noticed a gap in the market, and thought it was weird you couldn't buy it readymade. A few competitors have come on board since then, but at the time you really couldn't find it on the supermarket shelves.

I started experimenting with it, developing ideas and testing them on my family and friends to see if they would buy it, and the response was quite good. Soon they were stopping off on the way home to pick up their muesli. People weren't just buying it once in six months, they were purchasing it on a daily and weekly basis. There was a constant stream of sales, so I realised there was an opportunity to grow the business.

We moved into a share kitchen in 2012. I needed to get passive approval and food safety approval and couldn't really do that at home. The muesli was still being hand produced and hand delivered, so it was very local – pretty much Northern Beaches, Sydney's North Shore.

Then I got a contract to go into some of the Woolworths' small format stores and had to start using a contract manufacturer, so we moved out of the shared kitchen. As we took on more Woolworths' stores we've had to move to bigger manufacturers. In the past 18 months we've moved three times, which is quite a lot.

I snuck into Woolworths through the back door

We didn't need to invest in a huge amount of money to start the business, because we contract manufacture. I wasn't up for half a million dollars in machinery or have to invest millions of dollars in factory sites. Obviously, we had to commit to a certain amount of product, so we had to pay those up-front costs, but if I could kind of see the sales coming through, it was a little less daunting.

I got really lucky with Woolworths – they found me. A buyer saw me at a trade show and at the time no one was doing this product. The way I got into Woolworths is a bit like asking someone how you win Lotto. You need to have something new and exciting that they want. I kind of snuck in through the back door.

When I first started there were no real bircher muesli products in the fridge. Since then some other big players have come along and brought out similar products and they're creating more of a category, which has helped with sales as well. The tide is changing, people are looking for it in the fridge.

Competition isn't necessarily a bad thing. Large businesses have to spend to create space in the fridge, whereas smaller companies don't necessarily have to do that. I try and use that to my advantage and go in on their slipstream.

There are about 872 Woolworths stores in Australia and we're in about 250, across New South Wales, Queensland and Victoria. And we're in Caltex petrol convenience stores. Woolworths often has different buyers for each store, so the buyer you deal with in small-format stores is usually different to the buyer who is in a category in a big store – and they're often different to the dairy buyer. We started in small format stores to prove ourselves and recently redeveloped our mueslis, which got us into a lot more big supermarkets.

We're in quite a good phase at the moment. We've grown quite a bit over the past year and brought out a new fruit and vegetable yoghurt range in February. The yoghurt range is sort of like my children. I announced them in June, and our vegetable yoghurt was among the top three in the 'Best Yoghurt' category at the World Dairy Innovation Awards in Amsterdam.

I generate all the ideas. With the yoghurts, for example, most big manufacturing sites will have in-house development people who help put the technical side of the product together. Half these things aren't rocket science. Yoghurt has been made before, so I haven't been reinventing the wheel, I'm just looking at different ways to present the product.

We're leading the way

We were the first manufacturer in Australia to combine a vegetable in a yoghurt product. They're not completely mainstream yet, but they've been met with a lot of excitement and consumers really like them. It's a matter of getting people to find them on the shelves, which is a bit of an issue, because we're in the grab-and-go section at the front of store.

People might go to the grab-and-go section to get a Coke and then see my yoghurt and my bircher muesli right next to it. It's great to get those incidental buyers, but really, if you're trying to build your brand, you've got to get consumers looking for your product in shops. And even if they're looking for it, they've got to be able to then find it, because they'll lose interest quickly if they can't.

Achieving brand loyalty and making my product the go-to brand in the supermarket has definitely been hard, because I've been trying to build a brand and bring out two products that are not completely mainstream. Consumers would hear about our muesli, but would look for it in the cereal section, which is where you would obviously look for it.

I would get emails from people saying they couldn't find it. We're in the fridge and it was just our product in the fridge, there wasn't a whole category. We weren't doing an orange juice where people think, 'oh, I've got to get my orange juice', and they're thinking more about the product. With our muesli, people have to look for the brand and we're still not a huge player in the supermarkets in comparison to some of the big guys out there. But we're owned by me, so we're a bit different to the other products.

I don't think there are many businesses that are doing things that someone else can't do – you just need to find your groove and become well known for what you do. You can't think, 'I better not start that because someone else might do it', because then you would never start anything.

I'm in the final stages of studying for a Post Graduate Diploma in Business Strategy and Innovation at Oxford University, in the UK. I've definitely learnt a lot of things that help me look at business more strategically.

I don't get emotionally involved

There are a few things you feel when you're running a business, but scared is not really something that massively takes up my time. If it works, it works, if it doesn't, it doesn't.

I always get started and worry about the rest later. I've learnt not to ride the highs and lows of the business and take it all personally. Just the other day, we had really good news and some really bad news within the space of an hour. It's not do or die – it's a business. I don't link business success to my personal happiness.

There have been a lot of challenges that I've had to overcome. Shelf life has always been a massive issue, because I'm dealing with a time-precious product. It's a bit like a ticking time bomb, so I have to figure out better ways to get the product into stores as I go along.

That's probably become the biggest hurdle and we've had some pretty big learning curves around that. But I just go back to the drawing board and adapt my supply chain and try to get everyone on board to make it work.

Recently, some of our product was also date stamped incorrectly and we had to withdraw some stock. The manufacturer had to audit the entire process and take down two lines out of six. That was bad. It was a huge cost to the business. You've got to move on from those things fairly quickly.

Focus on what's right in front of you

I do my market research in the market. One of the benefits of being a small business is that you can be quite nimble and make decisions quite quickly, rather than having to go through market research and figure out if people are going to buy it. I also don't have that kind of money or anyone else to blame if the idea doesn't work. It's just me I need to apologise to and I'm very forgiving.

I can't go into battle with multinationals. They have millions of dollars behind them and an army of people. What do I have that they don't have? I have nimbleness, so I can adapt quickly; I can bring out products quickly. I try and build value into the story of the business and the person behind the business, which they can't do as much. You can go mad focusing on what everyone else may or may not be doing. You've just got to focus on what's right in front of you and work on that.

I get a lot of things done because I outsource manufacturing, warehousing and logistics, which dramatically reduces my points of contact. I have two or three people in each of those firms that I deal with and they manage their own teams. If I set up a manufacturing factory and managed it, as well as logistics, staff turnover and payroll, it would be really hard. Because I contract manufacture a lot of things, it is a bit easier to manage. I'm also quite organised, so I anticipate things happening. I try to give the manufacturers plenty of warning if something is going to change.

I've also got a graphic design agency for my packaging. I definitely invest in the packaging and presentation of the product. That's a big investment point for me.

I couldn't have done it without my parents

I've just moved out of home, but I stayed there for as long as I could. My parents have been really supportive. I couldn't have done it without them. I didn't take any money out of the business until last year and even then it's a basic salary. I still have a guilt complex sometimes that I take anything at all. I've never had a bank loan. I borrowed some money from my parents and the rest has been self-funded through babysitting jobs.

Mia's tips for getting started

• Start small, bite off more than you can chew and chew really hard. We had three major supply chain moves in three years and that was really exhausting, but I just kept going.

• Start while you're living at home. You can afford to take risks, because you don't have to earn money to put food on the table for your family. I can't underestimate how fortunate I was. I was able to transition from being a kid to being a kid with a business.

• You're more capable than you think. We're part of a startup revolution that's changing the way we do things and we're so lucky to live in Australia. Make the most of all your opportunities.

• Even massive companies have big problems – they've just got different sets of problems. Be flexible and really listen to the market; listen to your supply chain and the distribution network. If they say your product is not selling, you need to go into the store and ask them, 'why is it not selling? Where is it positioned and what can we change?' Sometimes they will like your ideas and sometimes they won't. You just need to keep looking at different ways to grow.

Management and leadership

As well as introducing the way she has developed an integrated strategy, Mia gives some wonderful insights into how she manages and leads her lean and nimble business. Notice how she doesn't do things the way her larger and formidable competitors do.

Mia plays to her strengths, and celebrates uncertainty by fearlessly having a go and experimenting. She controls her risks by securing the best suppliers and seeking to understand her customers' buying behaviours. And she manages her potential for loss by minimising her bets, and by structuring the business to ensure if she does fail, it is early, quickly and cheaply. Her management demonstrates that she certainly has found her groove.

153

Learnings I can take from Mia McCarthy

156

SARAH HAMILTON

CO-FOUNDER AND CEO OF BELLABOX

Sarah Hamilton and her sister Emily started their subscription beauty box business bellabox when they were living in different cities half a world away from each other. Today, Sarah says their success is partly due to their ability to embrace change and constantly strive to achieve bigger and better things.

My sister Emily and I launched a publishing company together when we were in Year 10 as part of a commerce project for school. The company was 'the Hamilton Family' incubator, because we initially ran bellabox and other companies through it before we realised we needed our own grown-up company.

Birchbox had pioneered the concept of the subscription beauty box when it launched in 2010. Emily and I were in quite well-paying jobs when we she came to me and said, 'why don't we do something like that?'

In the early days, we worked in our jobs while we planned for bellabox. I remember sleeping with my laptop, because I was in New York and my sister was in Singapore, so the time difference was hard. I'd get about three hours sleep a night, then log on at whatever time in the morning and do some more work on the concept.

This is how we got going

We funded the start with our own money and reinvested our earnings back into the business. It's great being an entrepreneur when you're 20 years old, because you're used to not having money. When you start in your thirties, you're used to the nicer things in life. We both switched to no salary and were supported by our partners.

The beauty box phenomenon was huge when we launched, so it was quite easy to acquire our first customers. We did a tiny bit of Facebook advertising. I was a bit upset that our first customer was a friend. It's hilarious now really. I felt like I had done all this work and then it was my friend's name came up as our first sale.

I think it almost helps that we didn't have a background in beauty. We were focused on the business and, of course, it doesn't do well until you deliver a great product and you're doing a good job of engaging with your customers. I think a lot of people have tried to have a business like this, but didn't comprehend the work required to get that little box out on a monthly basis. It's tough and there are days when you think, 'my god, I'm crazy', but you just push through.

The business is multi-faceted, so there were lots of areas that I'd never worked in before, such as logistics. Day to day, it was a very different experience than it is now. Now, it's a little bit more grown-up. We were servicing 300 customers when we started and answering all the social media posts ourselves. Customer service rang through to my mobile. We did everything.

The first website was put together after my sister read a software development manual, then we worked with some developers in Bulgaria to create it. At that point we wanted a little bit of this website and a little bit of that website. Then, once we got into it, we realised it's much more about understanding what the users are doing and we definitely looked to global leaders' websites for inspirations.

Website development and redesigns are never-ending. We've done a lot of work on the user experience and there are always things that need improving. I'm not going to point them out to you though and ruin the experience.

People of all ages subscribe to bellabox

Social media has been really big for us. We use Facebook, but we also look to other marketing channels. I have worked with print magazines and I like that it has been a successful channel for us. It's about testing various channels and seeing what works, but in terms of direct response campaigns, social media is still really important.

We try 'above the line' advertising and digital, because we really believe strongly in 'above the line' and more traditional channels. But when we're looking at our results on a weekly basis, it's super easy to see how social media works for us.

We have done some TV advertising, which is kind of unbelievable. We've just tested it regionally. It's something we wouldn't mind getting back into, but the company is constantly evolving and our customers evolve, too. Our database at the start was full of young beauty seekers, and now we have members who are in their eighties and girls who are 14. One channel can only target a portion of those groups. That's why we're always testing various channels.

We don't take ourselves too seriously

What we like about the concept of bellabox is that it brings a bit of luxury into everyone's lives. It's accessible. It's not meant to be intimidating, and it's something everyone can enjoy. So I think we were driven by that purpose of always being a little bit fun. We don't take ourselves too seriously.

I definitely think it has helped working overseas, because we look at our competitors globally, not just locally. We look at what other brands are doing and what we can do to improve the business. I don't think there has ever been a day, and there never will be a day, that I turn up and say, 'yup, everything's going really well'. It's more like, 'great, what else can we do here, here and here?' So it's constantly evolving at this point and it's driven by that lightheartedness.

We've been asked to start a number of bellabox offshoots and I suppose the furthest afield was Romania. We definitely want to keep growing the brand.

We're very clear on where we're authorised to sell the products, so we don't ship internationally – even if it's just a one-off event – unless we get great PR and we can tell the brand story. The brands we partner with always want to know what we're doing with their products, which is why we're really careful about it. Brands also have jurisdictions, so it is hard to say, 'all right we can ship it everywhere'.

You need an amazing team

We started off doing everything and now we're slowly outsourcing aspects of what we do. We've got a development firm in Singapore that we work with, but we also have an in-house developer. We have customer service contractors in Malaysia and the Philippines, but we also have our customer service manager in-house. If we get the right person managing whoever we're outsourcing, then we outsource wherever we can.

I still 100 per cent think you need an amazing in-house team. We look globally for people, because it helps to have someone who has a world view and has been thrown into a few difficult situations. That works for us. I don't think it would work for us if we outsourced everything. I still want the knowledge in-house, because I think there's so much for us to learn as a business, and it's not easy to say, 'this is how we do things', because we're changing constantly.

You've got to know what's going on inside the business, too. With development especially, you have to own the code and know that you have access to it all the time, and know the documentation is up to date. Say something happened to the firm that you were using? How would you be able to pass that work on to someone else?

Money is helpful but the right partners are vital

We've done two capital raising rounds. Our first pitch deck was hilarious, but we've learned along the way. I'm a conversational person. I don't really stand there with a presentation, going through it. I would rather talk to someone, make sure they've got the relevant information and find out what aspects of the business they're interested in. That has definitely been one of my biggest lessons when it comes to investors.

You just watch their eyes and look at what they're interested in, and you know. I stalk them on the internet before I meet them, so I know their background, their business, what gets their interest. It's about reading your audience and understanding what they want to hear about, and not taking too much time going through a deck.

Last year, Allure Media, which is owned by Fairfax, purchased 50 per cent of the business and our first investors bought slightly less than that. They really helped us focus and gave the business more direction. When you're doing everything, you want to move in a million different directions. They were like, 'you've got these competitors in Australia – don't do baby products, don't do men's products, don't do all these other verticals – be excellent at the women's products. Then, once you're big enough, worry about the other stuff that you can do'.

So providing that focus really elevated the conversation. I think we've been lucky to get great strategic partners that are coming into the business at the right time.

Accepting the status quo is dangerous

One of the hardest things about running a business is keeping up with growth. How do we keep the excitement around the product? How do we continue to engage our members? You don't get to come in one day and say, 'yes, we've done everything'.

Everything else, all the operational stuff, you can overcome, which feels like a blip on the radar. Never accept anything as the status quo. Never say, 'this is a great product and people want it for this reason'. I love chatting to potential partners and asking, 'what can we do that's a little bit different?' It's about making sure each and every box has a new level of excitement. It's not accepting that this box is perfect because we did all these things. You've got to say, 'what else can we do? What else are other brands doing out there that we can do something exciting with?

What are the important attributes of success?

Most of the time, we don't recognise that we've been successful at something. It's all about striving for more. There's no line that you reach and then say, 'okay we're here'. Every day we think, 'what else can we do?' I think striving for success is about constantly wanting something more. It's the ability to really push boundaries, collaborate with other businesses and brainstorm different ways we can work together. That works well for us.

We really understand our member needs as well. They like to be notified about something before they receive it, so we're careful about how we introduce partners and new products. The good thing about growing a company is you grow with your members. We look at our social media following and they've helped us learn along the way that you have to be upfront about something that's going to happen, because you want them to engage with the products.

Our audience is a close knit community and we want people to be members for four or five years, so we need to make sure we're listening to them. Our customer service manager does a lot of work on retention and she's always coming to us with ideas.

Membership numbers are also another important milestone in the business. I use the term 'glass ceiling' as something you push through constantly, but when you reach certain membership levels like 40,000, things go crazy. Those are the 'wow' moments. The next one I'm keen to crack is 50,000.

What do entrepreneurs ask you?

A lot of people are afraid to jump in. For us, it was a short conversation and then we just did it. We launched without the ability to subscribe, because we just wanted to launch and start improving on what we were doing. A lot of potential entrepreneurs get stuck on that. You need to be ready to devote yourself to a new company, a new idea. You almost need to push yourself to say, 'okay, as of tomorrow, this is the business idea that I'm working on, and I'm going to push myself until I make it happen'.

At the start we had a scattered approach to getting stuff done. And now, after reading a lot about it, I realise there's still so much to do. I really try to focus on the big things first – not check my emails all the time – and get outside the business. I think I'm one of those people who is happy to sit in the office all day, but building relationships has been really important to this business. If someone wants to meet me for a coffee, then I go and do that and that helps to motivate me even more. I always try to get the hard stuff done first every day and I don't avoid any work or get too distracted by everything that's going on around me.

NOTES

Sarah's tip for growing your business

You'll get to the point where you'll build a great business. It'll be a nice little money earner and all that kind of stuff, but if you really want to push your business, and you want to get bigger, you need investment. And it's not the money – although money's helpful – it's the partners who you bring on board. That has always been really important to us. How can we work with them? What can they do for the company as a whole? The money's helpful for growing, and we want to grow the business bigger than we could do on our own.

Management and leadership

Sarah draws out a number of insights from her successful capital raising. We can learn a lot about negotiation from her reflections. Firstly, she has prepared for discussions – she is clear about what she wants, the counter-party and their needs, as well as her alternatives. Notice how she deeply researches the counter-party (this could include their previous investments, ideal transactions, and typical exits). In this preparation stage entrepreneurs should also seek to understand what they are prepared to concede, and what their walk-away position is.

Secondly, we see that Sarah has focused on creating a productive environment for the negotiations – she has ensured each party is aware of each other's needs (hers being growth, capital and expertise; theirs being the nature of businesses and transactions).

Thirdly, Sarah is prepared to listen more than she talks (notice how she is alert to the body-language and reactions of the counter-party rather than just delivering a deck of slides). Successful negotiators will also seek to explore criteria, not particulars (for example, 'we are seeking a passive minority investor' rather than 'we are offering a five per cent stake without board representation'), and turning statements into questions (for example, 'are you able to take passive stakes in enterprises?'). Know yourself and your audience well before you pitch anything.

I THINK STRIVING FOR SUCCESS IS ABOUT CONSTANTLY WANTING SOMETHING MORE.

IT'S THE ABILITY TO REALLY PUSH BOUNDARIES, COLLABORATE WITH OTHER BUSINESSES AND BRAINSTORM DIFFERENT WAYS WE CAN WORK TOGETHER.

2.0

FOUNDER OF 99DRESSES

Nikki Durkin talks candidly about what she has learnt about herself and running a business since her startup 99dresses went into administration in 2014. She started the company when she was 18 years old. At its height she raised $US595K and had an office in New York City where her team processed over 1,000 trades a week. After having had time to reflect and rejuvenate, her next adventure is underway.

Even from a really young age I was always making and selling stuff. I started my first business when I was 15 years old, selling t-shirts online. I ran that when I was in class and my teachers would turn a blind eye as long as I did well in exams.

I learnt the basics of financial literacy running that business. I worked it out pretty quickly and my Mum helped with accounting.

I started 99dresses the day I finished high school. I'd thought about it for a few years and then just did it. I was doing university courses when I started and everyone said, 'you should be a doctor or a lawyer', but that just wasn't me.

The number one lesson my parents taught me was, don't get into something where you get paid for your time, because the amount of money you earn is limited by the amount of hours in the day.

I'm not knocking those careers, but for me the biggest risk was always being comfortable. I like the excitement of running my own business. I do it because I love it.

Yes, you have your ups and downs being an entrepreneur, but you create them yourself. Nothing really is an up or a down, you just assign meaning to it in the same way that people assign meaning to success and failure. At the end of the day, I'd much rather have all these experiences, because it has been fun and it's an expression of who I am.

I thought running a business was easy

When I started 99dresses, I was young and naïve, in a good way. It was really easy. I didn't believe it should be hard. I just had a vision and wanted to see it come to life. I was learning a lot and it was really interesting. Then the media started saying, 'you're this amazing entrepreneur'. I think I was targeted a lot because I was a good story. I was 18 years old, working in tech and there weren't a lot of females in that space.

I got wrapped up in this a bit, thinking, 'everyone thinks I'm so amazing, but it's really easy'. I didn't know any better. I didn't know what a startup was – I didn't know the rules or how to play the game. I just had ideas and executed them.

About a year after we launched, I had to decide whether to go to Y Combinator, in Silicon Valley. It meant I had to bring on a new co-founder and give away the same equity in the company that I had, and I had been working on this company for two years. A lot of people look at that and say, 'that's not right', but for me it was the opportunity to go to the best accelerator in the world and raise some money, and go and really execute my vision. The alternative was staying in Australia where I knew the market wasn't going to work for this business long-term – it was going to fail – and I would have zero per cent of nothing.

A lot of people look at Silicon Valley and think, 'that's startup mecca', and I used to be like that. I'm not trying to knock it at all, but I view it as a big bubble of startups, which can be quite dangerous if you're not exposed to people from different walks of life, with different experiences. I didn't want to live my twenties in a bubble, so I chose not to stay in Silicon Valley, but to go to New York instead.

The startup culture really does glorify raising money and going big or going home, whereas I think a lot of people just want to run their own business and that's fantastic. But as a society we're judgemental of people's decisions and say things like, 'you're not being ambitious enough'. Not everyone wants to be an entrepreneur though.

Whispering filled me with self-doubt

Before I moved to New York in 2013, Mum said, "Nikki, we're really proud of you, but your father and I thought you'd end up as a hippie on a horse farm, painting all day and growing your own vegetables, and there's nothing wrong with that, but you're just on a very different path'. I was creative and they figured out how to channel my creativity into entrepreneurship.

I always maintained a feeling 99dresses had plenty of money, and it did for several years. Our money lasted a really long time. Once we dipped below $100K I was like, 'okay, we don't have a lot of money anymore', and the purse strings tightened. Ironically, that was when things started going wrong and our sales dropped, and all these things would reinforce the idea that we didn't have enough money.

At the time, everyone kept whispering in my ear saying, 'you should be worried about this and you should be doing that' and 'startups are so hard'. I started believing it and it became a reality. I felt like my own worst enemy was myself and I was full of self-doubt. When I didn't have a reputation to uphold, I was just an 18-year-old kid giving something a go.

Entrepreneurs define themselves by their ability to persevere at all costs. It's like this struggle is your badge of glory. What I reflected on at the end of four or five years of running 99dresses was that I struggled way too hard and the harder I struggled the worse it got. Things worked best for me when I wasn't struggling; when I believed it was easy. I want to take that lesson into what I do next.

Just enjoy the ride

I look back on 99dresses and things that looked really terrible at the time – like my co-founders leaving or not being able to do a capital raise – I have a different perspective on now. I'm not so quick to judge anymore. If you're running your own business, you should just try and enjoy your journey – it saves you a lot of emotional pain.

I was so burned out after 99dresses that I wanted to sleep for six months, which was pretty much what I did. Next time, I'm going to be a lot kinder to myself and realise that I can put in all these hours of work, but I'm not going to be creative in that state. I bought into that whole culture of work, work, work, but it didn't get me anywhere.

When we closed the office in New York and I came home from America, Mum said, "Before you start anything else you should really take a look at your own beliefs about yourself and fix those". And she was absolutely right. I did an exercise where I wrote down all those limiting beliefs and it was a long list. I realised I was a product of my own self-concept in a way.

As 99dresses grew we felt successful, but then when it wasn't doing so well I felt unsuccessful. Now I define success by the amount of joy I have in my life. If you look at me objectively and say, 'what have you been doing in the past year?' I haven't achieved anything by society's standards, but I have done a lot of reflecting and I've changed a lot of thought patterns and mental habits, which has been a big deal for me.

I've discovered that I love coding

I've taught myself to code and I'm building a game. Every day I wake up and go, 'I really want to do this – this is fun and I enjoy it', so I feel pretty successful at the moment. Fishburners – the coworking space in Sydney – has given me a desk, so I've been working there and I've realised how much I missed the whole startup scene.

I want to build fun stuff and work with a fun team on my own thing. I've realised that I'm good at product-focused businesses and that's why I like the games. It's quite different when you're a woman as well. I mean I'm 23, I'm not exactly old, but if I was to commit to a big thing it would take up at least another five years of my life and then I might want to get married, have kids and settle down. So when am I going to go travelling and see the world? That's a big consideration for me.

When I had investors and employees I had to show up every day. I had a business where I had to physically deal with logistics on the ground – I couldn't just run it from anywhere in the world. For my next thing, I want a business that fits into my lifestyle, instead of me putting the business first and thinking, 'I'm going to have to live an unhealthy high-stress lifestyle in order to achieve this goal'.

Go with your gut feeling

If you have a business idea and you feel like doing something, just do it and don't worry about the outcome. It's really important to have a vision and gut level clarity that no matter what happens everything's going to work out fine. I lost that towards the end with 99dresses, because there was evidence that secondhand fast fashion wasn't a good market. There's just isn't great money in it. We had a really good solution to a problem, but it wasn't a good money maker.

A lot of young people say, 'oh, you're my inspiration', which is humbling when you don't necessarily live up to society's definition of success. I haven't sold my company for a gazillion dollars, but if young people can look at my journey and say 'you inspire me', then that's pretty cool.

Nikki's tips for entrepreneurs

• It's really important to listen to your own intuition about things. You can get so wrapped up in other people's advice. If I was to do it all again, I'd do it a lot more on intuition. But that's not to take anything away from mentors, I think they're fantastic, as long as you listen to the advice and then act, based on how that resonates with you.

• If you're starting out and you have a vision, and you think about it constantly then take action – do something. Get involved with other people and just do something that brings you closer towards that goal. Also, enjoy the journey, because then it doesn't matter if you're successful or not. Work with really good people and have a lot of fun.

• If you think you're running out of money, try not to panic, because it can start to affect everything around you. Stay calm and execute your plans, rather than looking at the money all the time.

• The more you give, the more word will get around that you're a nice person and you care about other people, and you're willing to help. I try to do that and so many good things come my way because of it. But I don't do it because I want good things to come my way. I do it because I think it's a reflection of who I am. I like helping people.

• When it comes to negotiating, you have no power if you're not willing to walk away. You can have all the negotiating skills in the book, but if you're not willing to walk away, then you'll get taken for a ride. If you think, 'it'll be fantastic if this happens, but I can do it another way if it doesn't', then you'll get a much better deal.

Management and leadership

Nikki appears already to have packed in more entrepreneurial adventure than many of us would achieve over a lifetime. She reminds us how closely success is related to the wellbeing and confidence of the entrepreneur. Confidence, however, cannot exist in isolation – it must be combined with knowledge, know-how and wisdom. Nikki has been reflecting on this, and it appears her leadership is growing with this mindfulness.

She realises that leadership is focused on people: on doing the right things, and creating multiple helping relationships. But it is also about committing to action, and taking responsibility for that action. You can do this in a calculative manner, but as Nikki notes – it is far more powerful if done authentically and genuinely.

STAY CALM AND EXECUTE YOUR PLAN

What can I learn from Nikki?

21

KATH PURKIS

FOUNDER AND CEO OF HER FASHION BOX

In China, Kath Purkis' manufacturers call her 'a lion'. The redhead with a tenacious business attitude started her first company Le Black Book when she was 21 years old. She learnt valuable lessons about doing business in China, which she has applied in her latest venture Her Fashion Box. Now she has her eye on her exit goal, but she's definitely not leaving her team behind.

I launched Her Fashion Box because I saw a huge opportunity and no one was taking it. Every month I saw women buying fashion accessories from online retailers. There was no community to it, no magazine, no beautiful box, no premium tissue. It was just stuff and there was no differentiation between any of the brands locally.

That's when I decided I wanted to launch into 'subscription commerce' and have a brand and a community behind this business, where we could give women something they looked forward to receiving every month. And I wanted them to be inspired by the founder behind the company. I saw a lot of e-commerce players, but few people were authentic in what they were doing. They were all about the sales and not so much about the experience.

We created hype around the brand

We raised capital from angel investors in Sydney to launch Her Fashion Box and we hit our first month's target within 48 hours of operation. Before we launched, I went on beauty forums with one of my employees and we created faux accounts to create hype around Her Fashion Box before we launched. We had five aliases, and we'd say, 'hey, has anyone heard of Her Fashion Box?' and we'd pipe in on another fake account going, 'yeah, I'm so excited about it'.

The real community on these forums then started talking about it and women began signing up for our emails, so we had about 3,000 names before we even launched. When I switched it on, all these women subscribed straight away. I'd also done a lot of pre-launch PR, but I'm pretty sure it was that growth hacking, being a bit weird on the forums and creating hype around the brand, that did it. That cost nothing.

It's just about being creative and putting your time into creating some hype. I spoke to early adopters and people I knew were already talking about similar products in the space. Then scaling it from there has been quite 'viral'. We're quite lucky in that a lot of our community will share the product on social channels. So many people just tell their friends. It's awesome.

We decided to launch into online fashion recently; so whole outfits are now available. Each month we bring out a new fashion collection. So we do our monthly boxes with the fashion accessories and magazines, and we do on trend fashion outfits in the magazine every month. We're trying to be best friends with all these young women.

You have to empower people

The first people we had in the business were interns. All my interns who stayed around me after the first few months became full time employees – a buyer, a customer services person; a brand director, a magazine editor, and a marketing person. We grew the team organically.

Moving forward we're looking to attract other amazing people, who are better than me at aspects of the business, so I sleep well at night and I know there's optimum output for everything they're putting together.

They always say, when it's your business, you're going to put more love and care into it, but I truly think if you empower people and they genuinely believe in the business – because they've stayed with you and hit goals – then they feel connected to the company beyond the pay cheque they're getting at the end of the day.

It's actually quite cool having people who have been with you from day one and you've seen them grow. We're like a family in that sense. I know that as we scale the business it'll be harder to have that, but if we have the right attitude within the team I feel like that will carry through.

I created something out of nothing

When you're first in your business, it's difficult to pitch to investors because you haven't got any evidence of what you've achieved. I was fortunate. I was able to attract amazing investors by showing them what I'd done before. I had already built Le Black Book and that had led me go to China and build a brand, be in the fashion industry, manufacture and do PR. Investors knew that if I could do that with no money and no backing, 'imagine what she could actually do with money and backing'.

We have tweaked our elevator pitch though. Our initial proposition was a subscription Her Fashion Box for Australia. We're now a global business, we're past break even and we've had two successful capital raises. We're in a really interesting stage where we're focused on scaling and on creating the ultimate fashion and beauty experience for all women globally.

That's not just a subscription fashion business. There's a rich data model behind it in the form of the style profile. Every woman who has ever bought from Her Fashion Box has told us her hair and skin colour, age, eye colour, body and hair type; whether she loves neutral tones or hates neutral tones; whether she likes neon, gold or silver.

This profile sits behind all of our subscribers. It means that when we send out our fashion boxes they are tailored to the woman who has purchased it.

Throw away the rule book

We have a 'no fail' policy at Her Fashion Box – 'you can try anything and I don't give a damn if you fail, but give it a shot'. If we stay within our comfort zones, we never grow.

Don't be complacent and do it by the rule book, because you're never going to innovate and your business will never grow if you're not pushing the boundaries. We're absolutely all about chasing something new.

In terms of our culture, the team works really hard. Sometimes we don't leave till 7pm or 8pm and it's not because of deadlines – they're not here for the pay packet or the cheque they get at the end of the month, it's about the journey. We're all about passionate people who are absolutely awesome at what they do. They've got the right values, they're dedicated to the business and they want to build something great.

When I was 18, I was so shy. You couldn't have got me to do an interview or give a lecture at uni, no way. And then when I had my first business, it got me out of my comfort zone and I've no doubt in my mind that a lot of the success that we've had in the business today is because I'm just willing to meet anybody and everyone.

I overcame my shyness by throwing myself in the deep end. Oh god, it was so horrible. I was doing these conferences and lecturing in front of 200, 18 year olds. I was just 22 years old and I was so damned petrified, but at the time I had one of my friends there and she was sitting in the audience and she was like, 'just do it' and I was so scared, I felt sick. But you know what? When I was out there and everyone was looking at me, I thought, 'that's right, I have information to share with you'.

I made jokes and now when I do speaking, I'm absolutely myself and I'll make the lamest jokes and people will just laugh – the whole crowd laughs. When I do guest speaking now I make sure that I engage the audience and I let them speak out, so although I might be there to talk about Her Fashion Box, marketing, branding or whatever, I always make sure I give them 'me'.

You don't have to go in your big high heels or your fancy clothes. It's absolutely not about what you're wearing, it's 100 per cent about how you carry yourself, how you speak and how you engage everyone. When I was younger I didn't get that. I thought it was all about how you dressed, what shoes and bag you had. I can't believe some of the stuff I bought. Now I'm like, 'why the hell did you spend all that? You were just hiding yourself'. I think that's part of growing up, coming into your own, being confident in who you are and having lots of self-love. I don't want to sound like a tree hugger or anything, but it's amazing really.

I was afraid to share my problems

One of the biggest things I found difficult in business was talking about frightening things. So if I had a problem, I wouldn't share it. If there was a problem I would just take it on as Kath's problem and be a CEO and get it done. That's absolutely not the way you do it. If you've got a problem, you're better off telling one or two people and they will help you solve that problem.

I'm so different now. If I've got a hurdle I share it straight away with somebody. That's far healthier than mulling over something for a week or avoiding something because you don't have the answer.

I'm a little bit unique and like to get the most out of each day. I only sleep for six hours every night. I wake up at 5am without an alarm clock and start emailing people and they're like, 'Kath's crazy'. Seeing my team grow, my customers grow, the business grow and the community grow is great. We had a really awesome weekend recently, where we took in more revenue in 24 hours than we usually would in a whole week. That's type of stuff is cool, but what's next? 'What's the next milestone? Let's keep going'. You can never become complacent and comfortable, because then it's boring. You want to challenge yourself and keep pushing forward.

I've got my exit plan

I'm definitely going to exit within two or three years. We've already been going for almost three years. My dream, post Her Fashion Box and having a substantial exit, is to start my own venture capital fund and invest in female-driven startups.

As a woman, raising money is hard and there aren't many female investors. You need a lot of money to do that, obviously, and Her Fashion Box is in a really fine space where I've already had a lot of interest in the business. I'm just going to keep scaling this baby until it's at a point where I've got, say, 100,000 subscribers a month and look at an acquisition with a company that would take it to 200,000 or 300,000 subscribers a month. So, yeah, I definitely have an exit role, absolutely.

I'm highly entrepreneurial and I love what I do every day, but I'd really love to be an investor in 10 or 20 businesses and spend an hour or two with an owner once a month and give her 20 contacts, and say, 'email this person', and obviously put in money, but also put in time to help accelerate their businesses. I love business and I love entrepreneurs.

We've got 15 people in the office now. I'm not just hiring people based on skills, I'm hiring people based on their values and if they want to be an entrepreneur in the future. If I can identify anyone who does, then I'm backing them.

I've got my dream beyond Her Fashion Box and I want the business to be successful, but ultimately I just want to be very happy. I love what I do and I absolutely adore my team – I can't wait to see them every morning. When I see them come in, it's the best feeling in the world, I'm like, 'yes, they're here, my tribe is here'. I can't wait to invest in them.

Kath's tip for doing business in China

When you go to China, it's really important that you can speak at least the basics of Mandarin. You need to show them that you really respect their business and you want to build the relationship. No matter who we do business with, I'll always learn basics so I can make the connection with them – and they really appreciate it. Some of these guys had never even seen a redhead before they met me. They call me 'a lion'. It's quite funny and some of them have come from provinces where there are few Westerners as well. And even the factory owners, they're great at doing what they do, but they can't translate. When they just say, 'hello', it's just the best feeling. It's so awesome. It's like, 'wow, look at you'.

Management and leadership

Entrepreneurs are a special kind of leader – they typically lead the organisation (which includes employees, suppliers, and advisors), but also the engagement with clients, customers and other stakeholders. Kath shows us how leadership is about more than motivation; and more than just ensuring that each person in the team is aware of their role and responsibility. Leadership is also about the entrepreneur's mindset, about their 'doing', their listening and learning, and (critically) about ensuring that they set the example for the team, the customers, and the stakeholders.

Kath has led the building of the organisation's culture and we all know that culture eats strategy for breakfast any day. Initially, entrepreneurs lead by doing, but as their organisations grow, successful entrepreneurs lead by letting others do.

DON'T BE COMPLACENT AND DO IT BY THE RULE BOOK, BECAUSE YOU'RE NEVER GOING TO INNOVATE AND YOUR BUSINESS WILL NEVER GROW IF YOU'RE NOT PUSHING THE BOUNDARIES.

NOTES

179

ALLI BAKER

CO-FOUNDER AND CEO OF WORKIBLE

Alli Baker and her business partner Fiona Anson came up with a way to change the way people look for work. The simple, but innovative idea was the inspiration for the website HireMeUp, which let users search for jobs to suit their daily schedules. Their latest venture Workible continues to grow, with more than 1,000 clients advertising jobs on their website to potential staff across Australia. Alli explains how they grew the business.

We started up about four years ago and as far as we know we were the first to start using availability matching for jobs. We thought if you could match love interests on a dating site, why can't you match availability interests on a job board. The first business was called HireMeUp and we had that for about a year. We had an overseas company develop the first website and it was built around matching days and times. Since then the concept has evolved a lot and grown to suit our clients' needs.

I really believe everyone deserves the opportunity to love what they do. Our business allows people to find a job that fits into their life and works for them, whether it's four hours a week or 80 hours a week. It's about customising your work life to suit you. Our business vision is to make that possible and I'm passionate about that.

We saw a niche and filled it

My business partner Fiona and I were consulting to a similar client, and because we lived close to each other we would commute together. In the car we'd have these long conversations and got to become friends, and one of the things that we were both struggling with was the need to find extra work. I was just starting my consulting practice, so I only had a couple of clients and I needed to find a part-time job that would fit around that schedule.

She had to work around her son's school schedule, as well as her clients. We had a similar problem and realised there wasn't an online job website that was based around time and days. So we figured we should build it! I was hesitant at first because I know nothing about technology or recruitment. Fiona had started businesses in the past so she had the confidence to take the chance. She was really inspiring and I jumped on the bandwagon.

I often say the first six months of starting the business was like having an affair. I had doubts about my own abilities and what people would think of the risk involved in starting a business that I had no experience in. Privately, I was proud of what I was doing, but at the same time the risk of judgement from people was scary.

I would tell them what was going on but I don't think I let on exactly how excited I was. That's the kind of tribulation the comes with being a young entrepreneur. It's imposter syndrome. Now I know there is no perfect pedigree or right steps it takes to become an entrepreneur. You just have fall into it, own it and try. Even if you fail, it's a great experience.

We've reached a point in the business where I'm extremely confident in where we're heading and I'm less afraid of what people might think of me. Exposing the ups and downs can be daunting, but I think it's our duty as entrepreneurs to share that with other people. The bad times are just as inspirational as the good times.

We know our strengths and weaknesses

When we did our first pitching event we didn't even know what a pitch was. There was a group of about 25 businesses pitching and the winner was going to be sent to Silicon Valley to develop their idea and attend a conference. Fiona is the more experienced public speaker, so I nominated her to do our pitch, and she practiced it all that afternoon.

When she got up to do the pitch she forgot half of what she was going to say. She sat down next to me and said, 'I'm so sorry, I just completely stuffed that up'. I told her not to worry about it and we couldn't afford to go to Silicon Valley anyway. But then she won! The pitch was so short and succinct it set us apart. We were over the moon.

Before we started Workible my background was in journalism and marketing, and those skills have hugely helped. I think other people see our lack of tech experience as a negative, but my media marketing background is exactly what you need to drive a business. You can have the best technology in the world, but if you don't know how to sell it, it's not going to fly. That communication strategy has served us really well and now we are working on a content strategy to support our digital marketing.

The first hire for Workible was in sales. Fiona and I really struggled with the sales process with our first website. Neither of us enjoyed it and we weren't good at it. We had to psych ourselves up every time we had to do a cold call, and when we got rejected it would shatter us. We realised the one thing we were really missing was somebody who was strong on sales.

Our experience with HireMeUp set us up well to know what we needed to do with Workible. HireMeUp didn't perform as well as we had hoped, because we didn't work on the innovation as strongly as we needed to. It taught us a lot about the market and other areas of business that we could take on with us. We constantly watch our cash flow and measure the results we get from our marketing. Fiona has a background in accounting and I am good at budgeting, so we can handle the financial side of things.

We're not afraid to take a risk on a new spend, maybe throw a few thousand dollars at billboard campaign, but we watch the result of that. We measure how much it's costing us per registered user and if that figure is up or down. Everything goes back to those metrics.

Workible is built on exceptional customer service

My background has always been in customer service roles or dealing with people. We know how we would want to be treated as customers, and I think that's something that our competitors have lost. They're resting on their laurels. People come to them without the need for much marketing at all, and so managing client relationships is not a focus. We customise our service for each client and make sure we are giving them great results. It's something that sets us apart from other HR startups.

One of our key clients was approached by another competitor and she came to me and told me all about it. I've had that happen multiple times with our clients, because they feel a loyalty towards us through the relationships that we've built. Competitors can beat us on price, but can they beat us on service?

183

JUST DO it. GIVE it A TRY

Customer service and marketing are key things worth building your knowledge on as a business owner. I've seen startups try to get as many clients and users as they possibly can really quickly. If you're not delivering a service those clients value, then you're wasting your time and money. You're better off growing slowly and then you can afford to start to scale. You know what you're doing right, you know what you're doing wrong, and you know what you need to provide to make a difference. As a startup you don't have money to burn, so if you can be smart with marketing and acquisition then you have a huge advantage.

The business is a flexible workplace

We're a pretty flexible employer. Since we support that industry we have to be. We expect most of our full-time employees to be here between certain hours, but if our staff have got something on or need to leave early we let them work around that. It's more about results and productivity than it is about hours spent in a chair.

We also keep check on what our staff want in their roles. We hate finding that people are bored, want to move elsewhere or feel uncomfortable in what they're doing. We encourage the team to be open with us and tell us if they need to be challenged or want to adapt their position.

In the two years Workible has been running we have only had one team member move on, and he wanted to go travelling overseas. That number is amazing to us and we really value the staff we have. We've been quite lucky in attracting a team that has been loyal to us and excited about what we do. They are willing to sacrifice a larger salary elsewhere to have the opportunity to work with us. We've been really fortunate and we give back to them with things like team nights and half-days. We always make sure everybody has a say in the business and we aim to keep things transparent.

As a small business you can't always afford to pay market rate or compete with other employers, especially in the tech world. It's so competitive to find talent, so you need other benefits that outweigh the salary. That represents what people look for in work today. It's not all about the money necessarily. People always talk about work-life balance and flexible options, but it's not easy from a management point of view. I don't think we have aspirations to be much larger than 20 people. At the moment we have about 10 staff, so I'd prefer to see our company stay nimble and small.

Go big or go home

I was lucky that Fiona was so sure about starting the business we dreamed up. I was hesitant, but now I would encourage anyone to just do it. Give it a try. People get so uptight and worry so much about the 'what ifs'. Stop worrying and just get on with it. The worst that can happen is somebody says 'no' or you fail. You might not make it, but the journey's going to be worth it.

At age 20, I would never have imagined I would be where I am now. That's not to say my business is out of the woods, but I would never trade the experiences that I've had. It's been hard and it still is hard, but it's so satisfying. 'Exposing the ups and downs can be daunting but I think it's our duty as entrepreneurs to share that with other people.'

How Alli reports and tracks performance

Alli reminds us about the importance of foreseeing and understanding the health of a business. As she notes, the most immediate and direct measures of an enterprise's wellbeing are sales and cash in the bank. Addressing these questions, even on a daily basis, would not be excessive. But as Alli and Fiona know, there are also broader ways to track performance. For example, they mention metrics, such as the early indicators of marketing impact, and performance against budgets and forecasts. Perhaps these are not posed daily, but these broader questions could be asked monthly or quarterly.

This could include *financial* aspects of the business (for example, 'is my income growing faster than my costs?', 'how many weeks' costs can I cover?' or 'how much money is owed to me and is it more or less than I owe other people?'), as well as *social* aspects (perhaps, 'are my employees happy to be working here?', 'are my customers happy with the quality of my product?'), and even personal aspects (such as, 'is my business worth more to me today than it was a year ago?', 'how does my income relate to my time spent in the business?').

Ask questions regularly and repeatedly; ask them of many different people (whether they're employees, customers, suppliers, family or advisors); ask them of formal data and informal insights and, most importantly, once you've asked, listen.

NOTES

CARRIE KWAN

FOUNDER AND CEO OF DAILYADDICT.COM.AU

When Carrie Kwan launched dailyaddict.com.au in 2008, the digital industry in Australia was in its infancy. iPhones hadn't been released and apps were about to take the mobile technology industry by storm. Eight years later her platform for discerning clients, who are looking for the best and latest experiences, has become a business with more than 100,000 members and offices in Sydney, Melbourne and New York.

I didn't want to start my own business until I discovered something I was passionate about and Daily Addict was the first idea that made me feel that way.

I was living in London and had lots of opportunities to travel to different countries. I wanted to know what incredible experiences existed in the cities I visited, so I could try them in the short time I was there. Locals always have insider information about the best restaurants and cultural experiences. Daily Addict is packed with that sort of information. It connects our readers with what's new and notable in their city, enriching their busy lifestyles one serendipitous experience at a time.

When I came up with the idea I couldn't stop thinking about it. There was a lack of this sort of offering in the market and there was a huge opportunity to bring it to life digitally. I came back to Sydney in 2006 and started collecting as many experiences as I could. I wrote a business plan and quit my job in an institutional bank to work on the idea full-time.

The early stages of digital adoption were so exciting

Digital was really in the early stages of adoption back then and it was an incredibly exciting time. eNewsletters and social media had so much potential to solve problems, make life easier and help conduct business in better ways. I found people in the industry were generous with their time and resources, and their input helped me get the idea off the ground.

My background is in corporate marketing for commercial services and I knew a lot of people who were hungry for the type of experiences I wanted to share. I registered Daily Addict in 2007, and we provided information by word of mouth in the first few months of operation.

I had a digital mentor who suggested platforms, apps and resources we needed to try. We had Facebook and Twitter pages, and it was interesting to see who came on board with those accounts in the early stages. First we had early adopters of technology, then a different wave of people – creatives – and then it became fashion and food industry people.

The first iPhone came out that year and we were approached by app companies that wanted to work with our content, so we developed what was probably the first lifestyle app on the market in Sydney. We didn't really know how it was going to affect business, but you have to be open to opportunities like that. It helped establish us as serious players in the digital media space, especially with agencies, premium lifestyle clients and 'early adopter' consumers.

In January 2008, we launched our eNewsletter with one feature story and a calendar of events for that week. I was self-funding the business out of my savings and investing around $30K to get it up and running – I just believed in it so much.

The business grew from out of my email marketing list and my own contacts list, and I did a mix of focus groups and surveys to research the market. Our business model has evolved as we've gone along, but I was much more naïve in my thinking back then. I stayed true to the business offering though, got advice from really smart people, and tested and trialled new things quickly.

We focused on high growth, member acquisition, and creating new products and channels. Any profit was reinvested straight back into the business. I worked from home for the first three years to minimise the overheads and we employed freelance staff, some of who are still with me. We had a steady stream of great clients, who began allocating more and more of their marketing budgets to digital as they could see the high levels of engagement we could achieve.

We started making a profit in year two and that's also when we started producing a dedicated city edition for Melbourne, and I began paying myself. I drew a minimal salary, which increased as the business grew. It's worth remembering that while your business as a whole might not show a profit, you can draw a salary as a business expense.

I have an insatiable appetite for digital

Daily Addict's user experience has definitely changed over time. It had to, because of the pace of technology, but also because people are much savvier now. We want to always be ahead of the curve in terms of what we're offering, so we're constantly introducing new components every few months.

We've gone through about five different versions of the website over the years. At the moment, we're playing with different widgets and seeing how to help clients navigate the experience better. We're getting feedback along the way and will be incorporating video into our next design change.

Making an impression on social media takes a long time. We have a lean team, so our time is precious. We make sure we look at what our objectives are, how we can measure activity, what sort of impact it's going to have on our business, and what type of return we're going to get from the resources we put in. Then we know if it's something we need to keep using or investing in.

Sometimes we get results early on that we can use straight away and sometimes they're lessons we can apply to the business further down the track.

Our audience trusts us

I think we're still here today because our content is highly relevant. We know our audience and we're able to keep them inspired, interested, and coming back for more. We've built a level of trust with them and we take a lot of pride in who our reader is – we really value and treasure those people.

We can also take an idea from concept to fruition quite quickly. We're always looking at different models and markets to see what's being done differently, and how we can bring that to our local market.

You have to be able to ride the highs and realise that at some point there will be lows in any business, but you need to be able to move on quickly from those – take your learnings and keep focused on what you're doing. I try not to give myself too much kudos when times are good and, on the flip side, I try to avoid blaming myself when times are bad.

We're trying to enrich people's lives and that's really important to me. I want people to get some value out of what we're providing, to be inspired, to share something and to help us build a database of experiences. That's what we always try to come back to.

We now have about 24 freelance writers and photographers based in Sydney, Melbourne and New York. We've grown a community of more than 100,000 people and each day we work to carefully and creatively curate stories about interesting people and businesses.

My door is always open

We have fantastic teams of people working for us and my door is always open to them. Actually, my door is always open to most people we come in contact with. Anyone who works at Daily Addict has to want to share his or her knowledge and contribute to the environment. We've built the business from the ground up, but the way we do things isn't necessarily the best way. If a member of the team knows a better way of working then we want to know about it. That's how we continually try to do better.

In 2011, Daily Addict secured $100K of cash funding, office support and IT development resources from a silent partner who valued the business at more than $500K.

If the timing is right, we can scale Daily Addict to cover any city with an upwardly mobile market, where time-poor, busy people are seeking discerning experiences. To grow quickly though, you need to be able to capture a market quite effectively and to do that you need funds. We also raised private capital in our second year, but I think we could have thought bigger in the beginning and got the funding on board sooner to achieve that.

The entrepreneur's path is usually a road less travelled and those you meet may not think the world needs your idea. Remaining confident and resilient is something I've always tried to project, but in private I have felt rather battered at times.

Your personal and business identity can get blurred so easily when you're working in a fast paced, 'always on' environment. One minute you are talking to clients or developers, the next minute sharing experiences with an audience or attending industry events. I try to keep track of each identity's weekly wins and also create mood boards for each of Daily Addict's persona.

There are a lot of tough decisions to make and stress to compartmentalise when you're running your own business – you rarely feel disconnected from its relentless needs. You have to believe in your idea and have the determination to find a way. Have conviction to go with your instincts when you're receiving lots of different advice and always be willing to ask more questions, and to listen.

Carrie's advice for startup entrepreneurs

• Put yourself out there and go to startup incubators and accelerators. They can help you road test your concept, provide founder mentoring and support and secure funding for your project.

• Test if there's a need for your product and if someone's willing to put down money for it. You might have thought you were targeting a demographic of, say, young girls and then realise that actually it's older women who are buying your product or service. Accept that there may not even be a need for what you're offering or that the market may not be large enough.

• Having a mentor is really important, because their experience can help you focus on the areas of your business that matter. In digital, there are so many opportunities and you may find yourself constantly pivoting or looking at different technologies to try and grow your business. It's easy to lose focus, so it's really important to have smart people around you, who have an unwavering belief in you and can offer you their support. These are the people who will help to keep you on track.

How Carrie reports and tracks performance

Carrie gives some important insights into how to report and track performance. Tracking performance should never be considered a drag, and reporting should never be just financials. For example, notice how Carrie and her team report and track performance with regards to their social media. Objectives are articulated, user activity is measured, and the impact on the business is understood. With this data the team can address the questions of return on investment or value for expenditure.

The team knows to look outside (to the customer), as well as inside (into) the business, utilising quantitative, as well as qualitative data.

Finally, Carrie and her team recognise that there will always be situations in which data and advice conflict. What can the team do about that? They can clearly differentiate data (objective information), insights (advice and findings), and framing opportunities (what it might mean for the business). Carrie is able to negotiate this complexity because of the clarity of her vision and because of her ability to ask questions, reflect, trial solutions, and scale when it's appropriate.

NOTES

TINA TOWER

FOUNDER AND CEO OF BEGIN BRIGHT

At the end of her first year of university, Tina Tower was told she wasn't suited for the corporate world. Despite this she went on to start her own business at the young age of 20. Her school readiness business Begin Bright, now has 24 franchises across Australia and continues to rapidly grow. She has managed to build her business while staying true to what really matters: living her ideal life with her family.

I opened my first business when I was 20 years old, in 2004. It wasn't until my second year of uni that I thought I'd start my own business and that's when I officially caught the business bug.

Straight out of high school I went into a business degree and then at the end of first year I was told that I wasn't very suited for the corporate world. It was suggested that I change to something more suited to my personality. I was a happy bubbly student, so I changed to a teaching degree. In my second year of teaching I started my business, a tutoring centre, to pay my way through university.

I loved teaching children, and thought the school system would be frustrating with so many kids in each class. My plan was to tutor until I graduated and then to go into a classroom. Initially, I was supposed to open just one tutoring centre, but I ended up starting an educational store, a birthday party centre, tutoring classes and school readiness classes all within the one big complex. Two years later, by the time I graduated, there wasn't a chance I was going into a classroom.

I discovered Robert Kiyosaki

I started going to Robert Kiyosaki seminars when I was 15. I think some people find religion when they're in that vulnerable teenage state – I found personal development. It filled me with the motivation and inspiration that I needed, because I was able to see what other people had created. These people had come from nothing and were able to build their businesses by starting early. I had no problems with working hard and sacrificing at that time.

I worked really hard when I was a teenager and had three or four jobs going through high school. In Year 12, I tried to save as much money as I could so that when I turned 18 I was able to get my own mortgage and buy a two-bedroom unit in Canberra. To me, property was a way of getting that freedom and the life I wanted to create.

A little boy called Owen started it all

Begin Bright focuses on school readiness and primary tutoring. Our guideline is helping to create happy, smart, confident children. The concept of school readiness wasn't a thing when I started.

There was one little boy called Owen, who came in for a tutoring assessment. We got the readers out so I could see what level he was up to. He was this big tough guy in Year 3, but when we got the book out he burst into tears. He said, 'I just can't do it. I'm dumb. Everyone thinks I'm stupid'.

He was just so defeated and had no self-belief. Every time I showed Owen something new he wouldn't even try. His default was, 'I can't'. I had this idea that we could start early and teach children good attitudes to learning. That way, by the time they started school and they encountered educational challenges, their default would be, 'that's alright. I don't know that, but I'm a good learner so I can pick it up'.

I wrote my own school readiness curriculum and licensed it to teachers around the country. They wanted a lot of business advice, so that's when I started franchising Begin Bright. We now have 24 franchises and we are on track to be at 30 by the end of 2015. We're going for 100 by 2018, which is a rapid growth plan.

Franchising for us was the best way to get Begin Bright throughout the country and maintain that quality standard. Every teacher is capable of opening their own tutoring centre. There's nothing stopping anybody. What sets Begin Bright apart is the culture that we've created, the support we provide and the vision that can't be replicated.

If we didn't have owners that were there in the centres and invested in that success, I don't think that same quality of education would be offered. Owners who are invested in their own businesses and have that level of care with their teams extend it on to the parents and children.

I work with great people

Up until the beginning of this year I had one other person on my team. We've now got three. I've got a general customer service manager, a fabulous EA and a business development manager. We have a totally open office and everyone knows what's going on all the time. It's a nice warm environment and there's a lot of flexibility.

Everyone who works here is a mum and I have a policy that you never miss a child's event. I don't think people should have to choose between work and family, you should be able to do both. That goes a long way in getting great employees.

We have a huge process for choosing franchisees. At the beginning, I felt like a begging dog rather than a sales person. I just had that insatiable need that people like me. Now I can afford to be a lot more thorough in my questioning. I always ask potential franchisees, 'why do you want to own your own business?' Their reason why is really telling. I want to know that when they get to that first stumbling block, which is absolutely inevitable, whether they're going to be able to get over it or not.

My business has been self-funded all along

I had $8,000 to start my own business enterprise and at the time I thought that was an absolute fortune. Then the gyprocking bill came and used up that entire budget. Luckily, I had a toy store, so I took the profit out of that and put it back into the business. For the first year or two I just chased my tail in that way.

I tried to get funding, because I knew that to grow as quickly as I wanted to grow we would need money or we would implode. The best offer I got was $200,000 for 50 per cent of the business, which was not anywhere near enough to tempt me. I knew that in a few years' time the business was going to be worth millions. I wasn't going to give away half of it for $200,000.

We made the decision that we would have to be self-funded. My husband took a promotion at work and I would get his income, pay all of our mortgages and bills, and we would have $200 a week to live on. The rest was put back into the business to market it and grow it.

Money has never been something I've had a lot of as a startup. When we started franchising Begin Bright it took a huge amount of capital, so it was like being back in the startup phase again. We poured all the money into the business and we had to sacrifice a lot to make it work. We've had to be really resourceful with marketing and PR, and that's what I've focused on.

In those first couple of years I just did as much as I could myself to save the money so we could keep pumping it back into the business. For example, the amount we spent on graphic designing was astronomical. At the end of the year, I realised it was too much so I went and did a community college course on graphic design, so I didn't have to pay someone to do it.

Juggling a business and a family is challenging

My husband has been a stay-at-home dad for a year and a half, so that has helped our household immensely. If you've both got to work it's really hard. I started franchising when my youngest was six months old and my other child was 18 months old. It was really tough.

Everywhere I went I had kids on the hip and in the sling. I felt like a terrible wife, a terrible mum and a terrible business owner. That lasted about two years. All the time I have women asking me, 'how do you do it with young children?' You've just got to accept that it's hard when they're little. It's going to be a tough couple of years.

At the end of my first year of franchising I nearly chucked it in. I was starting to talk to my husband about whether or not we should get divorced. We were having major issues financially, and we looked at our situation and thought, 'what's the ideal life for us? Are we really living it?'

We shook everything up. We sold everything in Sydney and bought five acres in Pottsville, just north of Byron Bay. Now we live on a farm and everyone has said that we can't run a growing franchise company from a farm. But I want to live my ideal life; I want to be able to create that for my family. After two years there, I'm happy to say the business has had year-on-year growth.

I wholeheartedly believe in my 'why?'

The key to my success is persistence and resilience. You need a big reason 'why?' If your 'why?' isn't strong enough, you just give up. I can see so clearly what I want Begin Bright to achieve. All of these thousands of children sitting in classrooms with smiles on their faces, feeling great.

I don't want any other child to come home from school and burst into tears because they feel like they're an idiot. I know there are huge problems in our world, but I think that's my problem and that's one I want to be able to contribute to fixing. I can work really hard to get that done because it's worth it.

I recently went to Uganda and it was an eye opening experience that helped me understand the issues that children face in the world. We're helping to build a school in Laos next year. Being able to make a difference in the world is really amazing and Begin Bright has allowed me to do that.

Tina's advice for aspiring entrepreneurs

Our world was designed by people no smarter than you. They are people that put their hands up, took their opportunities and had a go. Jump in, go for it, and create the world you've always dreamed of living in. It's far better to be in the arena feeling the pain of anguish and joy of triumph than bored on the sidelines.

It's not easy and it's certainly not a quick game, so do good, have your vision and goal in mind and every day strive for progress over perfection and you will eventually get there if giving up is never an option.

Tina's business DNA

Tina's decision not to accept an external investor into the business is impressive. Most entrepreneurs starting up initially rely on their own resources or personal credit, then seek grants from agencies or government, and the three 'fs' (friends, family, and fools) and only later seek the professional investors (such as high-net-worth individuals, angel investors, venture capitalists or the like).

The capital raised is sometimes in the form of debt that will repaid, but it is rare that security can be offered by a startup without assets. If debt is to be raised, terms such as interest rates, security, and the repayment of the liability must be agreed.

Another way to raise capital is via an equity raising, with part ownership of the firm exchanged for this capital. As Tina realised, at certain stages of growth this equity can be extremely expensive, as the capital isn't repaid – equity raising is like a marriage. If at all possible, it is far better for an enterprise to raise cash by self-funding its growth (perhaps by changing the payment terms or structures, or changing the business strategy), than through debt or equity. The right equity raising can transform an enterprise, but debt is cheaper, and self-funding is cheapest, but there are always trade-offs to be made.

THE KEY TO MY SUCCESS IS PERSISTENCE AND RESILIENCE. YOU NEED A BIG REASON WHY. IF YOUR WHY ISN'T STRONG ENOUGH, YOU JUST GIVE UP. I CAN SEE SO CLEARLY WHAT I WANT BEGIN BRIGHT TO ACHIEVE.

2.5

200

Photographer: Jennifer BaquingPhotographer: Jennifer Baquing

KATE KENDALL

FOUNDER AND CEO OF CLOUDPEEPS

Kate Kendall has had a few different entrepreneurial experiences with building community and connecting professionals at the heart of each one. Her first company The Fetch, a city event guide, was bootstrapped followed by a successful crowdfunding campaign. Then angel investors backed CloudPeeps, an online marketplace for top marketing, social media and content freelancers.

I grew up in a small town in England and moved to Australia when I was 10 years old. I wasn't exposed to many entrepreneurs growing up. Richard Branson was basically the only name I knew of as a child but didn't have the context of how to put into practice until much later.

When I was finishing my masters degree, I started to get more into technology and through that created Socialmelb, an offline gathering of people working in the digital space. From there, I started to get ideas of the types of companies I'd want to build and the kind of entrepreneurs I could relate to.

I quit my job and jumped on a plane

For a while, I was doing what I'd call 'tick box living'. I was the digital director of a magazine publishing company and living life how I thought it should be: collecting lots of stuff, being in a long-term relationship, saving for a house and working nine to five in an office.

In 2009, the relationship ended and it was a catalyst for me to make a lot of changes all at once. I quit my job in 2010, and headed over to San Francisco without knowing anyone there. It was somewhere I'd always wanted to go, so I didn't over-analyse my actions much, and bought a plane ticket at the last-minute.

For me, San Francisco and Silicon Valley represented the epicentre of the technology ecosystem. I wanted to be there, to be at the edge. When I landed, it only took me a few hours to realise this was home and that I wanted to do all I could to make it work so I could stay.

In 2011, I started The Fetch and was working on that for a couple of years. I lived in New York between 2013 and 2014, before making my way back to San Francisco this year.

I had the idea for CloudPeeps at the same time as The Fetch, but it was through building The Fetch that I really felt the pain point of struggling to grow it with limited resources. I couldn't afford agencies and hiring full-time folks was definitely beyond the budget. I hired a virtual assistant through a curated online service and thought it was life changing. Marketplaces had progressed so much, being quality-driven and locally-focused, that I got really excited about the possibility of CloudPeeps again.

I launched CloudPeeps at the start of 2014, and followed a strict lean startup methodology approach. The first site was a simple Twitter Bootstrap template and we were making money within five weeks. After a few months in, I started fundraising. I didn't know anything about how to fundraise before starting. I had read a lot of stories, but there's nothing like diving in and doing it. At first, I thought to target anyone who had the word 'investor' in his or her title. After a while, however, I realised there are many different types of investors for different stages, different focuses and with different investment theses.

I had no idea what amount to fundraise when starting out. At first the goal was quite low, more of a friend and family round but then it grew from there to become a seed round full of some incredible strategic investors and funds.

We raised across New York, San Francisco, Sydney and Melbourne. Fundraising is a lot like dating and when someone is keen, there's no messing about. You can tell if someone is interested straight away. Some investors say they even know if they'll invest before you've walked through the door. If an investor is unsure about you or less familiar with what you're trying to do, they will ask a lot of questions around market size or take a lot of time. It's a polite way of saying 'no' or 'not now'. They often like to hedge their bets until other people get behind you first.

There are a lot of challenges that come up when growing a company. Having a great team of experienced investors is very important. Previous founders who've had an exit make for great investors as they have the perspective and empathy needed to resonate with the position you're in.

Taking investment is a serious commitment. It was a huge learning curve for me as I went from having less responsibilities and lots of freedom with my first company to being a wrangler of many different viewpoints with the second. At first, I was trying to please everyone, but it's not sustainable as you get a lot of competing advice.

Being a startup CEO is knowing that you're going to have to make calls that not everyone agrees with. One of my investors shared some advice that really stuck to me. He said, "If you listen to and try to please everyone, you'll never succeed. If you listen to yourself, you might have a chance of success". At the end of the day, you don't want to regret the decisions you made and stood behind. You don't want to look back and feel you made mistakes because you sheep-herded everyone else's advice.

You also need to understand the startup stage you're at and focus on the right things. There's a difference between growing a business and operating a business. I'm a huge believer in having a sound operational and financial backbone, with strong legal frameworks in place. From there, it should all be about growth. You can spend time acting like a big company and doing big company things, like having lots of meetings and talking about what will happen in year five, but none of that matters if you don't have traction or product-market fit. You need to be scrappy. With that in mind, some of the founders I respect are those who have a bit of a cowboy mentality in that they're all about making things happen.

Building a remote work company

One of our formal advisors at CloudPeeps is Joel Gascoigne who is the co-founder and CEO at Buffer. The way that he's built his company culture and team was a huge source of inspiration for how I wanted to build CloudPeeps. He's been able to show that you can create a fast-growing company while also having a fun environment and living an amazing life.

We work remotely at CloudPeeps in that we don't have a central office. Right now, I'm working from my apartment – communicating with eight people who are based all over the globe. I absolutely love it and believe it's the evolution of work – to focus on productivity and output rather than counting the hours you sat at a desk. It's all about trust and communication. Even when I go to visit a large tech company's office in San Francisco, they are all chatting over Slack and IM. Work communication has gone online and 43 per cent of employees in the Bay Area are now remote. The future is here and I love it.

The freedom to work the way you want

One of the most rewarding things about creating CloudPeeps has been seeing people's lives change. We receive love letters daily from people saying that they quit their job, paid their rent or moved to a smaller city because of the work they've been matched with on the platform. CloudPeeps is especially great for those transitioning from full-time to being an independent worker. It solves a lot of the challenges, like finding customers, managing tax, organising client agreements and legal items.

All freelancers are vetted and apply to become a member of the site. It's been amazing to see the community and camaraderie between Peeps grow – the knowledge sharing is one of the biggest benefits of joining. The core value is all around people who want the freedom to work the way they want, from anywhere. It's about flexibility – to travel, work or start a side-project – and to do it while still having income stability.

Millennials now make up the largest component of the workforce. What we value most in our careers differs from other generations. We want to work on things we're passionate about and to continually learn. The saying goes that our grandparents had one job in their lifetime, our parents had five jobs in theirs, and we now have five jobs at once.

For companies, CloudPeeps also offers flexibility and freedom as business owners discover great talent to help build their communities and businesses. Much of marketing has moved on from the 25-page plan and annual media spend – it's much more agile and operates in real-time. Having access to a range of experts to focus on different channels, when you need, is a huge win.

I am CloudPeeps's power user

I'm always searching for talent on CloudPeeps to help me grow CloudPeeps. It's meta. I was the first customer and continue to test new features on the site – it's really helpful to have a first-hand experience. I have found Peeps to manage our social media, Peeps to help me do PR, Peeps to do content marketing, Peeps to moderate our community, and Peeps to help me organise events. Our matching specialist teases me that I'm always 'shopping for Peeps'.

I'd really like to see CloudPeeps become the number one place for the future of work: for skilled professionals to connect, find work opportunities and showcase their talent. It's the workflow infrastructure for people to create their online portfolios, find work, receive payments and manage their client relationships.

I learn from what other founders say

When I reflect back on how I've learnt the majority of my startup knowledge, it is from following what other entrepreneurs have shared. I follow them on Twitter, read blogs and catchup offline. I check out articles on Quibb and Mattermark and see what people are reading. Researching things on Quora, AngelList, Crunchbase and Product Hunt has also kept me up to date.

I like being first to try out things. I love trends and trying out new tools, and products. I was recently named the most influential Australian entrepreneur on Twitter and really, it was all down to being an early user and building an audience over many years. If you want to build products for the future, you need to live in it today.

Learning all about software development has also changed the way I work. I used to think work involved a lot of planning, strategy, documentation and communication. Discovering Scrum, continuous deployment, constant iteration and the agile manifesto reframed things for me. It really helped me to turn thoughts into action steps. So instead of, say, creating a marketing plan, I would now go on Asana and focus on a few key goals and the tasks required to achieve them. A lot of traditional companies spend a month talking about whether they should set up say, a Snapchat account. With a testing approach, you should just set it up, post some updates and see if it works. It's all about the actions you take right now. 'Focus' has become the buzzword of the day, but the steps you take at any hour of the day make a massive difference to your overall success.

Managing energy and time

One of the ongoing challenges I've encountered in my work is energy management. It was one of the reasons I moved back to San Francisco from New York – to live more comfortably and be protective of my energy. Sleep, exercise, close friendships and getting outdoors are important for me to be able to keep on doing what I do. It helps prevent burn out.

If you feel like you're getting burned out, reconnect with people, make changes to your business and be kind to yourself. Do the things that you feel like you're missing out on. Start by changing the amount and kind of work you're doing. For a while there I was working 100-hour weeks for over a year. Some weeks now I will work much less, at 50 hours, with a more structured day, but take weekends off.

I'd like my legacy to be around what I created and contributed to the world. I love helping people and want to do it in a scalable and authentic way. I really love building products and want them to speak for themselves.

Everyone says, 'be yourself', but it's hard to stay true to doing it, especially when you're being pulled in different directions. Don't get caught up in the game. Play your own game, be the best version of yourself, and live the life you want.

Kate's tip

Many entrepreneurs come to me with their ideas and ask for feedback. Undertaking plenty of market research is so important. You need to be obsessed with knowing what's happening – who else has done or is doing what you're trying to do. It's no longer enough to just be aware of local players – you need to have global knowledge. If you want to start something new – make it unique. Don't clone an idea from another country – it's so easy for the established original company to knock you out of the market once they launch locally. That's not to say, 'don't do it', but be really innovative and do something that's truly novel from the start or do it way better.

Kate's business DNA

To grow a business, capital will usually be required. This may be to cover initial investments, such as purchase of equipment or property, or to cover working capital requirements (essentially, to cover the timing differences between costs incurred and the ultimate revenue received).

Seeking capital can be dangerous for an entrepreneur, as they often find themselves spending more time on the raising than on their business. For entrepreneurs, this capital can be sought as debt, equity, grants or self-funding (by reinvesting profits). Each form of capital has its advantages and disadvantages.

Regardless of the capital sought, an enterprise can smooth the journey by ensuring the enterprise is investor-ready. Sophisticated investors will typically be encouraged by seeing an established and engaged advisory board, independent and external audits of performance, and (usually) lead customers or significant sales.

Understanding the expectations and previous investments of high-net-worth individuals or angel investors (who typically offer more than just cash, perhaps also promising marketing expertise or access to clients, and so on) or venture capitalists (promising everything, but often taking a large bite) is essential. Everything is negotiable in these transactions – so ensure you and your enterprise are investor-ready, that you make the time to engage multiple parties, and that you have the ability to walk away from unfair terms or parties. Sound easy? It's not.

WHEN I REFLECT BACK ON HOW I HAVE LEARNT THE MAJORITY OF MY STARTUP KNOWLEDGE, IT IS FROM FOLLOWING WHAT OTHER ENTREPRENEURS HAVE SHARED.

2.6

CARLIE ZIRI

FOUNDER AND DIRECTOR OF LIFESTYLE PROPERTY AGENCY & PINKCANDY ACCESSORIES

Carlie Ziri started Sydney Cove Property Agency when she was 25 years old and within three years went on to sell it for more than $1 million. She has since launched her second real estate firm Lifestyle Property Agency, and says researching the market, finding a great team and being passionate about what you do are vital ingredients for building a successful business.

When I left school I started a business called Sydney Promotions, which involved managing events. It didn't go very far, but it gave me a taste of creating something from the ground up. I realised early on that I don't fit into people's boxes – I never felt comfortable working for other people. After closing Sydney Promotions I started my career in the inner city property market and within five years I created the first property agency in The Rocks, Sydney Cove Property.

My business ideas just come to me. I literally got in the car the other day and thought of something new to do. Sometimes you've got to listen to your intuition and follow something that you're really excited about, and ensure you do the research. Then it's just putting the puzzle together to make it happen. I've always been able to just come up with things, saying that, probably only 25 per cent of them actually happen. To succeed you have to be able to make things happen.

The amount of research I do usually depends on the business. I made a mistake with one of my businesses and didn't understand the market or do enough research. Because I had such success with my previous business, this gave me a bit too much confidence and I ended up not pricing right, having a minimal margin on my products and buying way too much stock, so I struggled to make a good profit. It was a good lesson.

With Sydney Cove, I had spent my entire career in the market and was researching the idea for a good six to 12 months before opening. You've got to understand your market – know that there is a market – and make sure you know what your competitors are doing.

Once I've come up with a name, logo and overall brand then nothing stops me. I get the rest of it sorted, find a space, create the office, sort out phone numbers, web and IT needs, get all the legal contracts written and all the admin done – that's the grey stuff that no one ever talks about.

For me, it's the most exciting part of the business. I don't sleep much until it's done, but then you get through that first 12 months and things get into a groove. That creation part is like having a child – watching it grow is amazing. When it's profitable and it's running that's when I get bored and want to try something new.

I self-funded my latest real estate business Lifestyle Property Agency. My first venture didn't cost much to set up at all. I had savings and I borrowed a little funding from family. I've never done a capital raise. All our money goes back into our home or our businesses. If we ever need to grow, we borrow against our assets.

It's a great feeling when your hard work pays off and you have a million dollar business. We reached that in the first year at Lifestyle. I'm at the point now where I need to probably set new goals, because I'd like it to be a $5 million business. Then you've got to make that decision – are you willing to take on another three or four staff and go that next step or do you keep it manageable and create something different?

Our next target is $3.5 million and we're probably on target for that next year. You've definitely got to adjust your targets every 12 to 18 months, depending how the business is growing.

I didn't take a wage from Sydney Cove until it was profitable. Even now after tax I only pay myself a very minimal wage. But at the end of the year we just pull out what we need, that's kind of how we roll. And from an accounting perspective it's better to do it that way than to pay yourself a huge wage.

When you're starting a new business you do have to put everything into it. We lived on tuna and noodles for the first couple of years, but we were really lucky with Sydney Cove, it was profitable quickly, so was Lifestyle.

I used to work seven days a week

In the first 12 months of starting Sydney Cove we were the only agency in The Rocks in Sydney. I think people could see what I was achieving and they were attracted to it, so building an amazing team was really easy. This time around it has been harder, maybe because I'm not physically doing the deals and I'm not in the office as much. I've really struggled to find sales staff, but the market is tougher now.

With landlords and tenants we had 500 clients, and 12 staff at Sydney Cove. I felt like I needed to say 'yes' and deliver to everybody. It was difficult balancing everything. I had to make sure it was financially viable, then I had to come home and cook dinner. I poured everything I had into it and my health suffered.

I probably bowed out a little bit earlier than I would have wanted to, but I needed to for my health and I'm glad I did, because I don't think I would have been able to remove myself from it. You've got to set those boundaries when you first start.

I wanted to work on the business not in it

With Lifestyle, I wanted to work on the business not in the business, and thankfully I've been able to do that. I know for the next couple of years, at least until my youngest child starts school, my business can't be my soul focus. So it is about doing something that isn't going to take every hour and every day. There's no way I could have been a present mother with Sydney Cove, because that was too intense.

Is there a secret to being a mother and running a business? Yes, get help.com! I currently run the agency, publish the lifestyle guide and have an online fashion accessories business called pinkcandy.com.au so I needed help this time. I have someone three days a week who comes in and helps with the children and that allows me to work and be sane. It would be almost impossible to run a business without someone helping you with the children.

With my youngest child, I've worked since giving birth earlier this year and I'm so much better for it. I outsource pretty much everything at home. I haven't always done that, but thankfully I'm able to do that now and that allows you a life, which I'm grateful for. In my business, I outsource most things that aren't too dollar productive, things like databasing and admin work. We also outsource some of our accounts, but we do everything in-house that's dollar productive.

We've got 10 staff and we manage about 450 apartments. This time I invested in someone to build the rent roll – that's the soul of a property agency and is a register of rent income due to landlords – so this time I don't actually have to get involved in any of the day-to-day real estate transactions.

When I was personally involved in building the rent roll, particularly with our property management clients, I felt responsible for the owners' mortgages. We had really high-end properties of between $2,000-$5,000 a week. If one week's rent was missed it really affected their investments. I wanted to make sure that service levels were high and vacancy levels were low, and that my team was happy. It was hard to manage all that as well as sell property, run the business and be there for the team. There were many sleepless nights.

I think everybody goes through that with their first business and then, if given the opportunity, you know what to do differently the next time. This time it was basically about putting the right team together and making sure they all had an incentive to stay, because it's really hard to keep them.

I work on keeping the team motivated. I do all the branding and new ideas, create our *Lifestyle Guide* – our bi-annual guide about living in the city – and do all the fun stuff. I've been a little bit savvier about marketing, costs and budgets as well. It has been a lot easier this time.

When I think about what I'm really passionate about though, it's the inner city. I love Sydney – I love the city and I love the market, so that's probably where my passion is, rather than in real estate itself. I also think Lifestyle's a really great brand. Creating that brand was a lot more exciting than the concept of actually starting a real estate agency this time around. I'm also hoping to give back and contribute to society with my next venture – that becomes important, too.

I'm on social media every day

From a branding perspective, I think social media is really important. Our Lifestyle Properties' profile page is full of pretty pictures of beautiful houses. That actually gets more likes than the really interesting stories. At the end of the day though, it's just about getting your brand in front of as many people as you can.

I try not to post too much. People can overdo it sometimes. With Lifestyle Properties we post once a day, and with Lifestyle Property Agency we'd probably do it three or four times a week. We've got a lot of followers on Twitter and Instagram, because it's not just about property, we are in a city where the focus is on lifestyle and what's happening. We're developing a good following by tuning into that. We're attracting a different demographic.

We used to only really market to the inner-city and to investors. Just being on social media though, we're finding lots of younger people who are wanting to buy their first investment. We wouldn't have come into contact with these people before. They're aged between 21 and 35, whereas in the past our demographic was 35 to 70.

I'd say 40 per cent of our likes are international. We get a lot of enquiries from Dubai, Asia and Europe. They like our Lifestyle Properties page, which is about worldwide properties and we tag different countries into those. People like the page, because they can relate to the city and then they become familiar with our brand.

I like empowering my employees

I've changed a lot over the years when it comes to managing people. I've learnt to listen to the team and hear their feedback. I've always got ideas, but I try to empower my staff, so they can come up with ideas. I want them to grow.

I sometimes recruit people by following them on LinkedIn and watching what they're doing. Trying to find the right people is hands-down the hardest thing about business. If we had an influx of staff I would be creating many more businesses.

We always give the team a great night out, but a lot of the time we reward them financially, because that's part of the reason why they're in the business to begin with. We offer incentives sometimes even for admin staff. I'll always say, 'if we can get the business to this point by the end of the quarter, you'll get a bonus'.

Retention is just as important as new business

Retaining and keeping business is all about delivering your promises. In real estate, there are a lot of people who talk the talk, but don't deliver. If you call someone and say you've got a great tenant or buyer, you need to deliver on that. You also need to return calls – all calls! That's probably the best way to retain clients. You've got to focus just as much on retention as you do on new business. We also really look after our tenants, because they often become landlords.

I'd say probably 70 per cent of our business is referrals. I don't go anywhere near my old client database now, because I'd hate to spend over a million dollars for a business and then the old owner goes and opens up down the road again. I created that brand to begin with, so I want to see it thrive.

I'm really honest. I think in property that's really hard to come by. I could have doubled the amount of income I've made over the years, had I been less than honest. But I will tell people the truth rather than making quick money. As a result, people have stayed with me for many years, because I've always looked after them and they know they get a straight answer from me.

PEOPLE HAVE STAYED WITH ME FOR MANY YEARS,

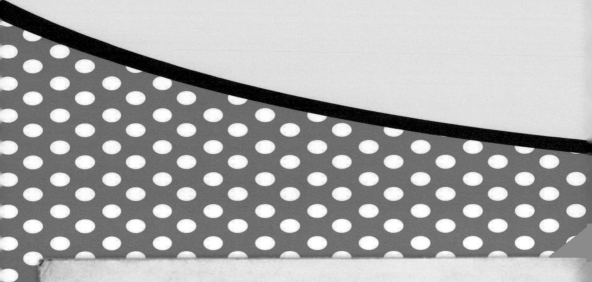

Carlie's tips for startup entrepreneurs

• Look after your health, manage your lifestyle and realise that although business is exciting and empowering, it's not the only thing in life. I learnt the hard way that money absolutely does not make you happy.

• Get a mentor – someone who can guide you through the next 10 years.

• Don't take shortcuts. Make sure all the contracts you sign have options. Don't get caught up in five-year deals with less than average products and suppliers.

• Start a spreadsheet of everything that needs to be done in the first year, so you can use it again when you start another business. Then, next time round, all you'll need to do is tick the boxes.

BECAUSE I'VE ALWAYS LOOKED AFTER THEM AND THEY KNOW THEY GET A STRAIGHT ANSWER FROM ME.

Carlie's business DNA

Serial entrepreneur Carlie brings particular clarity to the challenges of building a business. Notice especially her advice to be 'on' not 'in' your business. She advises you to seek a helicopter view of the business and its strategy rather than being always in the mess of tactics and operations.

To do this the entrepreneur must take as much care of themselves as of their business. Balancing everything (particularly over a long period) is too difficult, so it is important to decide where that help will be most beneficial. Your business has a life beyond you (you can sell it, divest or close it down), and you should also have a life beyond your business.

27

MARNIE SHANAHAN

FOUNDER AND DIRECTOR OF THE NEW KID PTY LTD

Internships have received a lot of negative publicity in Australia and around the world in the past few years. Marnie Shanahan had both good and bad experiences when she herself was interning during her studies in Sydney. She was inspired to create change and build a better system for interns while promoting legal, beneficial internship programs. Her website The New Kid has recently launched and Marnie's journey as an entrepreneur has just begun.

The New Kid is an internship job board and career site that helps young Australian's transition into the workforce. I want young people seeking internships to be able to access all of the details and facts upfront so they can understand the quality of the role before applying, so I've focused on making the platform as transparent, succinct and simple as possible. I also wanted to build a positive environment where we really celebrate the businesses that are doing the right thing, engaging interns ethically and mentoring them.

In 2014, I was the joint winner of the Rexona Clinical Women's Agenda Pitch Off. At the time I was obsessing over the business idea and was working on it in my spare time while I had a full-time job as a web and social media coordinator. The competition brief really hit home to me – a business idea or concept that was going to shake up the way Australian's live and work – and that's the point of The New Kid: to disrupt the industry and make change. Once I won the competition it became a reality for me and gave me the motivation I needed to get started. I quit my job and went for it.

My personal experience inspired the website

I really care about intern equality, because I've been in that position of wanting your dream career and feeling helpless when it comes to getting that experience, so I know exactly how it feels. It all started in my last year of university when I did four unpaid internships on top of having two casual jobs and studying full time. That's what you have to do these days to get experience to help break into the workforce. It's just crazy what some companies are getting away with. I interned for one company and had an awful and exploitative experience. I was doing admin and data entry and there was no structure or education to contribute to my degree whatsoever.

Then, on the flipside, straight after that my second internship was amazing. The directors went out of their way to make me feel like I was part of the team, so I never felt like I was just the unpaid help. They did so much for me and in return I learned so much. I'm still close to them and they're always at the end of the phone. I realised that was what an internship should be, especially if it's unpaid. I thought, why isn't there an internship job board that actually helps people like me identify the good ones from the dodgy ones?

The further I looked into it, I realised there were countless internships advertised every-day that were exploitive, but young people like me had no other choice than to apply and cross their fingers that it would get them a foot in the door. If internships are going to continue – and they are – then I think someone needs to really focus on them and create a dedicated and relatable space for young people looking for work experience. If no one's going to do that, I will.

I'm working it out as I go along

I was the kid out the front of my house selling oranges, busking in the streets, and making earrings to sell at local markets, but as far as actually starting a company I'm a fish out of water. I'm teaching myself everything by going to classes, reading, watching lectures online. I've got a notebook that I scribble everything in to keep track of what I've done, need to do, and things I learn along the way. Even two months ago, I didn't know what I know now. All the skills I have developed at university studying photomedia and in my job as a web coordinator have contributed to my success so far. They've been the building blocks that have led to the place I'm at now. One benefit of starting my own company is that I have no choice but to teach myself how to do everything and I know that I have a hand in each part of the business. It's daunting, but it's also very rewarding.

I'm the type of person who jumps in with both feet and learns from my mistakes – and I've already made plenty. There's no shame in that for me, it's all about learning. Before I started, a couple of business advisors told me I needed a long, thorough business plan. I didn't know what the concrete plan was, I just got going. If I'd listened to them I would still be trying to write this huge document and it would have already changed 20 times. I got straight into it and I am picking up things along the way, but that's the way I learn and it's working for me.

I'm in the mindset where you do and learn as much as you can yourself, then you see how customers react before you put too much money into an idea. I'm content with the decision to go slow and learn it all myself. The big mistake would be to turbocharge, spend a fortune and lose it all.

Marnie's business DNA

Marnie has articulated one of the key skills and joys that entrepreneurs manage – active learning. They don't only 'do', they also 'become'. Entrepreneurs are continually being challenged, shocked, frustrated and battle-hardened (as examples). But the successful entrepreneurs are also continually learning, building new businesses, and becoming new people. If an entrepreneur one day finds that they have ceased to learn, perhaps that's the signal that they should find something else to do.

NOTES

What I learnt from Marnie

I'M CONTENT WITH
THE DECISION TO GO
SLOW AND LEARN IT
ALL MYSELF.
THE BIG MISTAKE
WOULD BE TO
TURBOCHARGE, SPEND
A FORTUNE AND
LOSE IT ALL.

IT'S NOT ABOUT IDEAS IT'S ABOUT MAKING IDEAS HAPPEN

WHAT'S THE dREAM?

224

www.inspiringrarebirds.com

www.inspiringrarebirds.com

www.inspiringrarebirds.com

www.inspiringrarebirds.com

www.inspiringrarebirds.com

phronesis.academy

ENTREPRENEURIAL LEARNING IN ACTION
email info@phronesis.academy

www.inspiringrarebirds.com

www.inspiringrarebirds.com

www.inspiringrarebirds.com

www.inspiringrarebirds.com

www.inspiringrarebirds.com

www.inspiringrarebirds.com

www.inspiringrarebirds.com

www.inspiringrarebirds.com

END

....THE BEGINNING

RARE BIRDS

229

Special thanks to Dr Richard Seymour

NOTES

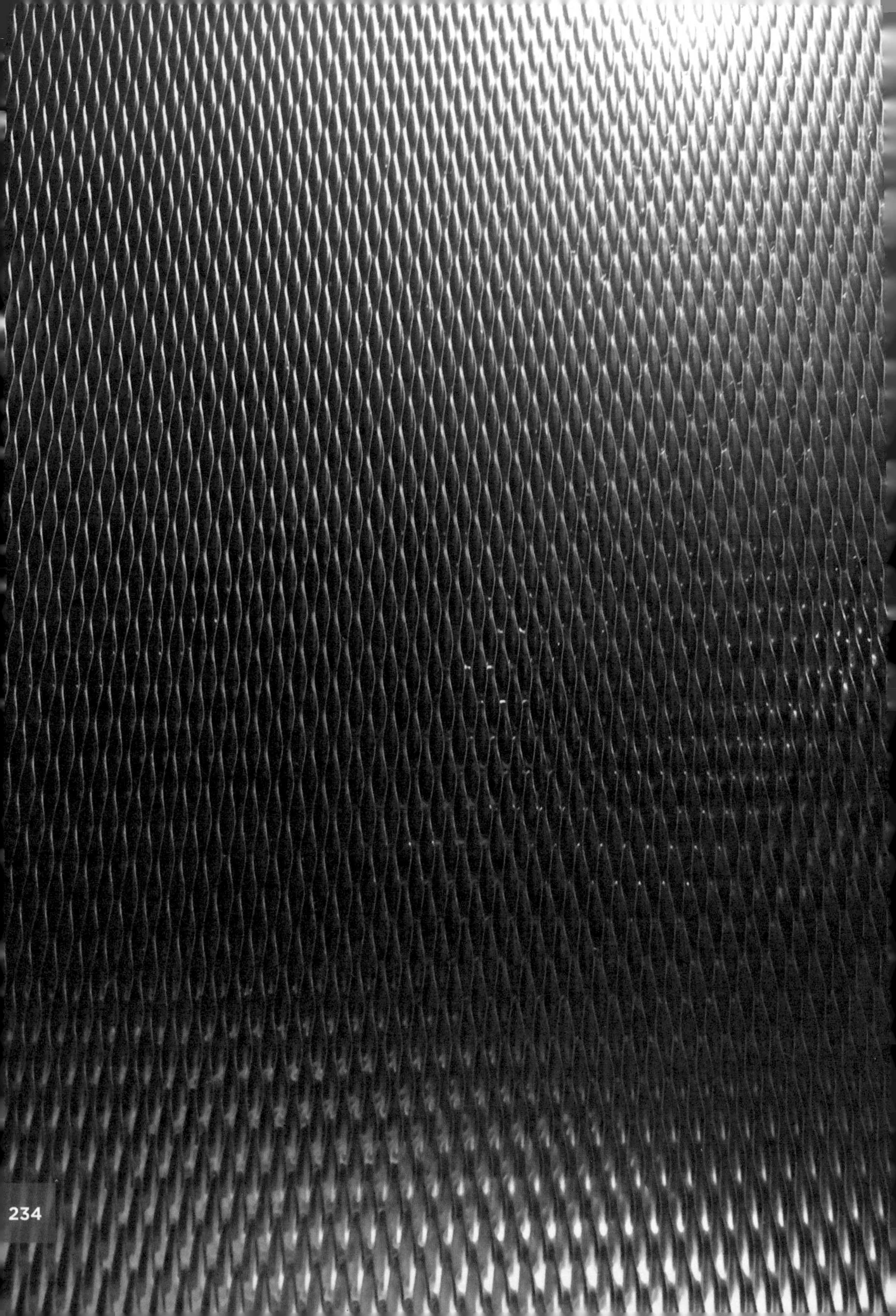